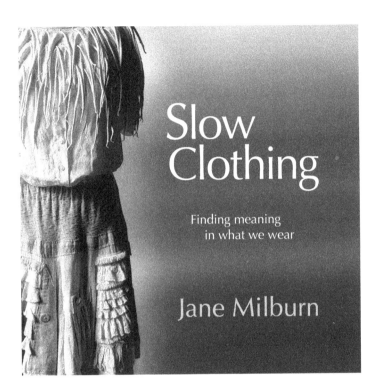

Slow Clothing

Finding meaning
in what we wear

Jane Milburn

This History Skirt carries a story of how it came to be.

It was created by Jane Milburn in 2012 with lace offcuts
leftover from childhood garments made by her mother
Elizabeth Capon, as well as pieces of discarded linen and
silk garments restitched for fresh life as a gored skirt.
It affirmed the potential for individuals to create new
clothing from old, for pleasure, reward and sustainability.

This book is dedicated to grandchildren of the world, including my own, whose future we protect by living lightly on Earth in our everyday practices.

FOREWORD

Planetary health is about safeguarding the health and wellbeing of current and future generations through good stewardship of Earth's natural systems, and by rethinking the way we feed, clothe, house, move, power, connect and care for the world. Since the middle of the 20th century, there has been a dramatic acceleration in human enterprise. Population growth, technological advances and rising incomes have combined to exponentially increase the footprint of the human species on our planet.

By most measures, human health is better now than ever before in human history. However, to achieve these health gains the natural environment has been exploited at an unprecedented rate– examples include rising carbon dioxide emissions, forest loss and fertiliser use. In discussions of sustainable development, much of the focus is on rethinking our approach to energy generation, housing, urban development, transport and food production. Our approach to clothing is often overlooked as a sustainability challenge.

I recall the care and attention that my mother and grandmother took with our clothes in the 1960s. Most of our clothing was made locally, and often hand sewn by family members. Many delicate items were carefully hand washed. We didn't own a tumble dryer. Any clothing damaged was carefully repaired. Items of clothing were handed down between the children and later passed on to relatives or neighbours. By the time clothes made the rag basket, they had provided a lot of service. In just a few decades, we've seen profound changes in our clothing culture. Clothing has seemingly become just another disposable item in our highly consumptive society.

'Fast food' is a familiar term in everyday conversation. 'Fast fashion' is now emerging as a term to describe quick, easy and increasingly disposable garments available at every turn. In this book, my sister Jane Milburn documents changing clothing cultures in Australia and other high income countries. She draws attention to the rise of synthetic fibres in clothing production, changing approaches to sourcing, caring for and wearing clothes, and emerging mountains of clothing waste. The book offers practical suggestions for a more reflective approach to the garments we wear in everyday life.

In the interest of planetary health, it's time to embrace Slow Clothing.

Tony Capon, Professor of Planetary Health, The University of Sydney, Australia

INTRODUCTION

Slow Clothing is the antithesis of fast fashion. It is a way of thinking about, choosing and wearing clothes so we have meaningful connection to them.

Today we are subjected to incessant marketing which creates a mindset where we believe we must have the newest/brightest/best to compete and appear successful. Often we are left feeling insecure and unfulfilled by this consumer cycle.

When we order a look from a catalogue or shop, our needs are met on a superficial level but we soon have a hunger for something more substantial.

I grew up in the time before globalisation enabled cheap commodities. That was before wasteful disposable clothing, when people had skills to make things and were attached to them on an emotional as well as a functional and aesthetic level.

My earlier work was around farming as the source of fresh food and more recently I began exploring the parallel story of clothing and natural fibres. I learned that two-thirds of our clothes are made using synthetic fibres and that research has shown these plastic fibres are shedding microplastic particles into our ecosystem and oceans. We, *the wearers*, need to know more about such things so we can respond through our everyday choices.

I've become a material activist, a craftivist, championing a more natural and hands-on approach. When we re-skill we have agency—to darn a hole and mend a tear to keep clothes in service. As we grow our skills, we solve problems in our wardrobe and explore our creativity.

As society evolves into post-consumerism, now is the time for bricolage—the practice of creating something from natural resources on hand as a way of living lightly while gaining attachment to things that bring meaning to our lives. We are multi-dimensional, we humans, and our looks are just a small part of our essential being.

Slow Clothing is about individual expression and personal connection to what we wear. We stitch to make our own mark on things, and to be mindfully engaged and productive. In return, we are satisfied and liberated from commodification and an endless search for meaning through buying more things.

We have finite resources on Earth and everyday choices that show careful and considered use of those resources are required if we are to sustain our individual and collective future.

Jane Milburn, Slow Clothing pioneer and founder of Textile Beat

Slow Clothing is a philosophy.

It is a way of thinking about, choosing and wearing clothes to ensure they bring meaning, value and joy to every day.

— Jane Milburn

Chapter 1

PURPOSE

Why we need to dress with conscience
Ethical issues: increasing consumption, changing fibres, waste, modern-day slavery, loss of skills and knowledge

Clothing, like food, is essential for health and wellbeing. Our clothes do for us on the outside what food does inside. They protect and warm our bodies, and influence the way we feel and present to the world.

Dressing is an everyday practice that defines and reflects our values. We are naturally attached to clothes on a physical, emotional, even spiritual level. We are particular about what we wear because we want to look good, feel comfortable, reflect an image and belong.

Yet almost all our garments are now designed for us and we simply choose from ready-made options based on our age and stage of life, work, status and spending capacity.

Unless we deliberately choose to step off the fast-fashion treadmill, we are trapped in a vortex with little thought beyond the next new outfit—without consideration for how we can engage our own creative expression, energy and skills to what is already around us.

At this point in history, the global fashion industry annually produces 100 billion garments[1] and that may accelerate with automation as sewbots[2] begin producing one t-shirt every 22 seconds.

Two-thirds of new clothing is made from synthetic fibres derived from petroleum. These are effectively plastic. They may never breakdown. Research has shown they shed microplastic particles into the ecosystem with every wash[3]. Other research has found microplastic[4] appearing in 80 per cent of drinking water, the likely source being everyday abrasion of synthetic clothes, upholstery and carpets.

The trillion dollar fashion industry, it has been said, is the second-most polluting after oil, although the source of that assumption is unclear. Electricity, food and transport would also rate highly. A recent *Pulse of the Fashion Industry* report[5] did make fashion's sustainability abundantly clear however, rating it 32 out of 100, with much room to improve its social and environmental performance.

A scathing assessment was provided by recycled menswear pioneer Geoffrey Small in Sass Brown's 2010 book *Eco fashion*:

> Bad for the customer, bad for the worker, bad for society and bad for the environment, fashion today is one of the Industrial Age's biggest human failures. Dominated by large global corporate groups and their sponsored media who encourage a dream lifestyle of selfishness, apathy, superficiality, greed, sex and drugs … Fashion is indeed a massive human, social and environmental disgrace in need of a paradigm shift. That shift has begun … the mighty rules of sustainability are now making themselves known to all.

Slow Clothing is not a book about fashion or the fashion industry. It is a holistic approach to the clothing choices we make each and every day in what we wear and how those choices may impact our health and the ecosystem in which we live. It is about self-empowerment through resourceful thinking and individual actions.

For some time, I have pondered the difference between clothing and fashion. Is fashion clothing or clothing fashion? When is fashion no longer 'in fashion'? If we wear things that are old, they can't be fashion so they must be clothing? Variously we have slow fashion, ethical fashion, eco fashion and sustainable fashion. Yet fashion by definition is ever-changing, so how can it be slow or sustainable? Fashion is also used to describe the latest style of hair, decoration or behaviour.

From this perspective, I have arrived at the concept of Slow Clothing as philosophy—a way of thinking about and choosing clothes to ensure they bring meaning, value and joy to every day.

Slow Clothing is about thoughtful, ethical, creative and sustainable ways to enjoy clothes while minimising our material footprint. Slow Clothing manifests through 10 simple approaches—think, natural, quality, local, few, care, make, revive, adapt and salvage—detailed later in this book.

For me, the Slow Clothing philosophy has been distilled through a lifetime association with natural fibres inevitably stitched together during the past five years through my purposeful social enterprise, Textile Beat. I dress, observe and interpret, based on my values, experience and kansei.* Read about my journey in Chapter 2.

I am not alone. There is a growing movement towards making, mending and modifying garments for ourselves to wear because it provides connection. Chapter 3 shares creative insights from my Sew it Again project as well as from other makers who were part of The Slow Clothing Project. Chapter 4 shares a manifesto of ways to survive and thrive in a material world, while Chapter 5 provides simple upcycling ideas.

For the past few years, I have written about our clothing story in blogs and journals. By way of introduction, here's a 2016 abstract.[6]

A Japanese word that covers the meanings of sensitivity, sensibility, and intuition in English.

The transformational shift during the past two decades in the way we source, use and discard our clothing has major social and environmental implications. Clothing is at its cheapest due to international companies accessing low-wage labour in developing nations, which now produce the majority of garments sold in Australia. Consumption has risen as prices have fallen…Second-wave feminism in the 1970s which saw Western women embrace education and professional careers while diminishing domestic duties— along with the busyness of modern lifestyles— have contributed to the loss of sewing and other life skills such as growing and preparing food. Since consumers need to eat and dress every day to survive and thrive, the turn back to localism and self-sufficiency evident in the slow food movement is sparking growing interest in more hands-on approaches to clothing and textiles.

Historical context

Since the melting of ice caps brought us into the Holocene era about 11,000 years ago, *Homo sapiens* have survived and thrived on Earth. In recent decades our per capita use of energy and resources has escalated sharply. We appear to be entering the Anthropocene[7] era in which human activity is markedly impacting our ecosystem and climate.

It is only in recent millenia that humankind has progressed from hunter-gathering food and wearing garments that were handmade from skins and fibres to now sourcing what is needed from convenient and economically efficient global industrial supply chains. In earlier times, people valued their clothes, having a few quality items for 'Sunday best' alongside many well-worn hand-me-downs for the rest of the week.

Our clothing consumption has incrementally increased since the emergence of ready-made fashions in the 1920s and '30s. Ready-to-wear became mainstream in the 1970s, liberating Western women from sewing. Now in developed nations, the process of shopping and buying clothing in stores or online provides recreational therapy as well as limitless supply for owning and (sometimes) using.

Yet in becoming accustomed to quick, convenient purchasing, we have distanced ourselves from the details of where our food and clothing actually comes from. Surveys suggest some children believe yoghurt comes from plants rather than animals, and that some adults even believe chocolate milk comes from brown cows![8]

Slow Food, Slow Clothing

Coming from a background in agriculture, it is second nature to consider the resources that go into food and clothing. Regenerative agriculture—as we would prefer all agriculture to be—values soil and nature as part of an ecosystem that requires good stewardship to produce into the future.

We need farms to have fresh food and natural fibres. Yet as our food systems have industrialised over time to bring supply-chain efficiencies and cheaper prices, we—the eaters—have become more passive and dependent consumers of industrial production.

In *The pleasures of eating*[9], American author and farmer Wendell Berry described eating as an agricultural act. Similarly, I say, dressing is an agricultural act if you want to wear natural fibres rather than plastic ones.

Author Michael Pollan, *In defence of food*, defined an eater's manifesto: eat food, not too much, mostly plants. Similarly, I define, a wearer's manifesto: wear clothes, have few, mostly natural fibres.

The Slow Food Movement emerged in Italy back in 1986 as a response to fast food, and in defence of local seasonal food traditions and unprocessed wholesome choices. As a pushback against fast processed food from industrial supply chains, we have seen resurgent interest in home cooking and sourcing more ecological, nutritional and sustainable food for health and wellbeing. We see it in our backyards, urban and community gardens, farmers markets and community-supported agriculture networks (such as Food Connect[10] in my city of Brisbane which provides local food direct from farmers).

Eating fresh whole food is the best defence we have against chronic diseases known to be linked with obesity. Yet by all accounts, much of the manufactured food found in supermarkets is high

Our clothes do for us on the outside what food does inside.

They protect and warm our bodies, and influence the way we feel and present to the world.

— Jane Milburn

in calories and low in the nutrients our bodies need. Society is now literally bulging through over-consumption of easy, yet ultimately unhealthy, food choices: two-thirds of the Australian population is identified as overweight or obese.[11]

In their book *Planet obesity*, Garry Egger and Boyd Swinburn link obesity with consumerism and climate change. They suggest we can help ourselves by living a low-carbon lifestyle, changing our way of thinking about how we live as much as our actual behaviours.

Commercial interests influence us in unhealthy ways. The British documentary *The men who made us fat*[12] revealed the truth of consumption habits that see us overfed while undernourished. In the series, Jacques Peretti exposed how corporations devise tactics to sell us more and more unhealthy addictive food. It is troubling to see socially irresponsible businesses exploiting human weaknesses and addictions for commercial gain.

In a similar way, Slow Clothing is arising as a grassroots response to industrial production of

The United Nations' Sustainable Development Goals for the world and its people.

cheap fast fashion which many now consider to be unethical, unsustainable and unsatisfying. Effortless shopping from a catalogue of ready-made clothing engenders a culture of cheapness and churn, rather than care and connection.

There is a significant disconnect between the consumption drivers of modern economies and the reality of living in a finite world. Popular culture offers convenience with fast food (take-away coffee, bottled water, food in disposable packaging) and fast fashion that requires minimal effort from the user. Efficient supply chains have made consumption of many things now quick, easy, cheap and disposable.

Let's face it: business makes money out of selling us things—endless snacks, gadgets and pretty things—we do not need. Sometimes the 'ethical, sustainable' branding is just another way to sell a slightly improved version of the thing we already have. I've seen 'handmade' printed on takeaway sandwich boxes, if you please.

With the risk of dangerous climate change acknowledged by nations worldwide through the United Nations' Paris accord and the Sustainable Development Goals in place, we can all contribute by living lightly and engaging sustainable skills and strategies. Activities such as growing, caring, sharing, recycling, making, saving, upcycling and reusing may take a little more effort and commitment but it is the amalgamation of individual choices to slow consumption that can make a difference in the world.

In *Clothing poverty: The hidden world of fast fashion and second-hand clothes*, Andrew Brooks said:

> From an environmental perspective the individually responsible decision is to choose to shop less often, wear clothes until they are worn out, and then repair or recycle them within the household or replace them with locally produced goods. Slowing the rate of clothing consumption by buying fewer higher-quality clothes is a far more environmentally friendly approach than continuing to buy fast fashion and donating excess clothes.

Clothing in or out of fashion

In developed nations, most of us are spoilt for choice with every conceivable item of clothing available in a plethora of colours, styles and sizes ready for our consuming pleasure. New styles arrive every week now, not every season.

We humans are materialistic by nature. According to *New Scientist's*[13] Alison George we have five stages of engagement with goods—desire, buy, use, reject and toss. It is our ability to imagine how new things might change our lives—our transformation expectation—that drives us to acquire them.

We may purchase our identity according to the brand message that grabbed our attention from the rivers of print, screen, digital and social information flowing our way, tapping into insatiable yet contrived desires for more.

Returning to those earlier thoughts about fashion versus clothing, Professor Kate Fletcher from the University of the Arts London's Centre for Sustainable Fashion offers the following interpretation. While clothing meets our material needs, fashion emerged to satisfy non-material needs for participation, identity, freedom and to signal wealth and social status. In her book *Sustainable fashion and textiles: design journeys*, Fletcher said:

> Fashion linked us to time and space—and catered to emotional and social needs. Hence where the fashion sector and the clothing industry come together—in fashion clothes—our emotional needs are made manifest as garments. This overlaying of emotional needs on physical goods fuels resource consumption, generates waste and promotes short-term thinking as we turn our gaze from one silhouette, hemline and colour palette to the next in search of a new experience. It also leaves us feeling dissatisfied and disempowered, because external physical possessions are unable to satisfy internal psychological and emotional needs, no matter how much we consume.

Do we need to follow contemporary mores when we know that having more does *not* translate into living better? Why attempt to keep up with ever-changing trends when we know this is leading to huge consumption and waste of resources? In the same way that most manufactured food in supermarkets is unhealthy, cheap fast fashion is unhealthy too. As we understand the value of slow food, we are learning the value of slow clothing.

Conscious consumers are now looking beyond visual appearances and understanding that planetary health is at stake here—our clothing choices don't just affect our own health, they affect the health of others and the health of our planet.

Ethical dilemmas

Economist Juliet Schor in her book *True wealth* said the most revealing fact about the contemporary apparel market was clothing could now be purchased by weight, rather than by the piece, and the price may be less than rice or other foodstuffs. Schor wrote:

> The production system drives businesses to use natural resources at hyperspeed and the consumer system makes the resulting products redundant almost as fast. It's a recipe for disaster.

While we cannot easily influence the way our clothing is made (unless we make it ourselves), we can become more informed and change the way we buy, use and discard it.

I stepped into this arena as part of an active search for meaning. Through independent research and experiential learning, I sought to understand our clothing story in a context broader than fashion: a lifestyle context that includes everyday practice and individual creativity.

I love natural fibres and noticed their presence in shops and on people was dwindling, while the overall volume of clothing was increasing and little of it was locally made. I went looking for information, made observations and considered the landscape. In thinking creatively and seeking agency, I embraced a Slow Clothing philosophy.

The ethical issues around clothing culture as outlined below are intertwined. We buy more clothing because it is cheap. It is cheap because global supply chains exploit workers and resources. It is cheap therefore we treat it as disposable—why mend when we can throw away and buy new?

1. Increasing consumption

Every thinking person knows endless consumption is wrecking the planet. Our Earth is finite. Infinite consumption is not possible in a finite world.

Women's clothing price index

Cheapest since 1989

Figure 1. Women's clothing is the cheapest it's been in 28 years.
Source: Alan Kohler, October 2017, ABS, CommSec

Clothing consumes resources (water, energy, nutrients and petroleum), uses toxic substances (chemicals used in fabric production, dyes and plastic byproducts) and pollutes further at the point of disposal.

Women's clothing is at its cheapest in 28 years, according to Australian financial commentator Alan Kohler[14] (Figure 1). Plummeting prices are a key driver to increasing acquisition.

According to *Choice* magazine[15], Australians annually spend an average of $2300 each on clothing and footwear. About 92 per cent of clothes sold in Australia are imported. Clothes can be produced in developing nations at a fraction of their real cost because environmental and labour protection laws are less strict. Contaminated river systems, people poisoned by these pollutants, or dying in factories in foreign locations, are largely out-of-sight and out-of-mind for most consumers.

Apparel fibre consumption per person

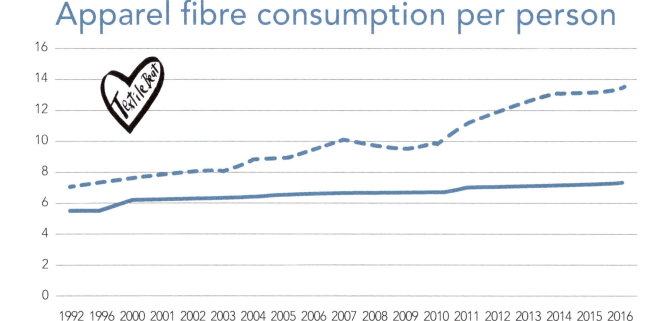

Figure 2. Apparel fibre consumption per person. Sources: Food and Agricultural Organisation World Apparel Fibre Survey 2013 and World Fibre Reports 2011-2017.

Individual consumption, based on the global average, has doubled from 7kg two decades ago to nearly 14kg now, according to data I compiled in Figure 2 from the Food and Agriculture Organisation World Apparel Fibre Consumption Survey extrapolated with annual World Fibre Reports.

The solid line shows the steady growth in global population over the period while the dotted line shows consumption rising steadily except for a dip during the global financial crisis. While there was exponential growth from 2010-2013, the past few years have seen a levelling off in demand, perhaps due to growing awareness of the environmental impacts of clothing excess. Somewhat encouragingly from a planetary health perspective, the 2020 outlook *The Fibre Year*[16] summary suggests 'a slowing of fibre consumption in advanced economies that had previously shown above-average demand'.

While Figure 2 provides a useful overview, it does not reflect the disparity in consumption between developed and developing nations. Australasians are the second-largest consumers of new textiles— averaging 27kg each—after North Americans (37kg each), according to 2015 information from Textile World (see Figure 3). Arguably Australians are using up to four times more clothing now than two decades ago (in 1995 the average was 7kg per person). We are well ahead of Taiwanese (23kg each), Western Europeans (22kg), South Koreans (21kg) and Japanese (20kg). These figures contrast starkly with less affluent nations of Africa,

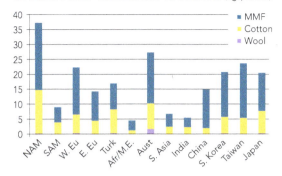

Global Final Consumer Demand (kg/person)

Figure 3. Global Final Consumer Demand in 2015. Source: http://www.textileworld.com/textile-world/ fiber-world/2015/02/man-made-fibers- continue-to-grow/   Note: MMF is manmade fibres.

the Middle East and India where the average per person is only 5kg.

Inevitably in future, we can expect consumption trends in emerging economies such as Africa, South America and Asia to mirror those in developed nations and further magnify the problem.

When British journalist Lucy Siegle wrote *To die for: Is fashion wearing out the world?* in 2011, she said that every year about 80 billion garments were produced worldwide and textile production had doubled in the past three decades. Consulting firm McKinsey[17] indicated that in 2014, global production jumped to 100 billion garments annually. That is a 25 per cent increase in just a few years. In both cases, the precise source of these figures is unclear, yet the upward trend is troubling.

Global apparel fibre consumption

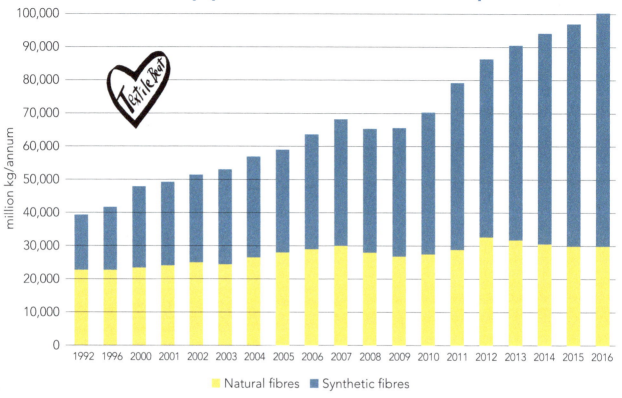

Figure 4. Global apparel fibre consumption. Sources: Food and Agricultural Organisation World Apparel Fibre Survey 2013 and World Fibre Reports 2011-2017.

American journalist Elizabeth Cline provided another perspective in her 2012 book *Overdressed: The shockingly high cost of cheap fashion*, stating that Americans consumed nearly 20 billion garments a year (that's 62 garments each).

2. Changing fibres

In earlier times, clothing was relatively scarce and made from natural fibres—cotton, linen, wool, leather and silk. In about the 1930s, the arrival of synthetics like polyester and acrylic, derived from petroleum, provided cheaper alternatives. By the year 2000, synthetic fibres filled half the market need and there has since been a further dramatic shift. In little more than one decade, synthetics now represent two-thirds of new clothing and textiles—far surpassing natural fibres. For more details, see Figure 4.

Microplastics

My concern about synthetic fibres is that they are plastic. As part of global research looking at shoreline pollution, ecologist Dr Mark Browne found synthetic clothing sheds microplastic particles (<1mm) which eventually flush into oceans to contaminate the food chain and the planet. Browne said ingested and inhaled fibres carried toxic materials: that up to one-third of the food we eat is contaminated with this material. The study[18] published in *Environmental Science and Technology,* found:

> Experiments sampling wastewater from domestic washing machines demonstrated that a single garment can produce >1900 fibres per wash. This suggests that a large proportion of microplastic fibres found in the marine environment may be derived from sewage as a consequence of washing of clothes. As the human population grows and people use more synthetic textiles, contamination of habitats and animals by microplastic is likely to increase.

Browne suggested[19] this microplastic problem may be Asbestos 2.0 with potential to become an environmental and health disaster. Synthetic clothes, being essentially plastic, may never break down in the environment or buried in the anaerobic conditions of landfill.

A *Primary microplastics in the oceans report*[20], prepared by the International Union of Concern for Nature, found almost all microplastic in the oceans came from land-based activities, with the laundering of synthetic textiles said to be a key source.

Further disturbing new research[21] has found microplastic present in the majority of our drinking water. Scientists indicate the most likely source to be the everyday abrasion of synthetic clothes, upholstery, and carpets.

Land, water and energy

Many argue that synthetic fibres provide a substitute to resource intensive natural fibres. There is increasing competition for agricultural land and water from the world's expanding population and urban sprawl. Natural fibres are grown on farms that also produce our food. While natural fibres do have an environmental cost in the production phase—using land, water, nutrients, energy and chemicals—the fibres are biodegradable. In *New Scientist*, environmental researcher Joseph Poore wrote about the relative requirements for fibre production—with one hectare of land able to produce 300kg of wool or 2000kg of cotton, while synthetic fabrics require essentially no land.[22] It is vexed, however, because wool is usually grown in the rangelands without irrigation and instead of land, synthetics use non-renewable fossil fuels that are polluting nature through the bioaccumulation of microplastic. Which is worse?

In terms of water use, United Kingdom sustainability group WRAP (2012) said the cotton used to make a pair of jeans required about 10,000 litres of water to grow, while other groups have said it takes 2720 litres of water to make a t-shirt—as much as one person drinks over a three-year period. In his book *The coming famine*, Julian Cribb (2010) said growing 1kg of wool (enough for a suit) required 170,000 litres of water.

Although dwarfed by the United States, China and India in terms of volume, the Australian cotton industry has made serious strides in improving its sustainability credentials since 1997 through the introduction of a Best Management Practice program which includes environmental auditing and water-use efficiency measures.

Adoption of integrated pest management systems and cotton plants modified to resist insect pests have enabled significant reduction in pesticide use, down by 90 per cent.[23] Improved water management has seen water use reduced by 40 per cent.[24]

Only two per cent of the world's cotton is grown organically, in high-altitude parts of Texas in the United States, India, China and Turkey: to the best of my knowledge, no organic cotton is grown in Australia. Organic materials are certified by the Global Organic Textile Standard (GOTS).[25]

Cotton and linen are plant fibres (cotton from flowers, linen from flax leaves) while wool is a protein fibre from sheep fleece. All three have much less embodied energy than synthetics, requiring 10, 55 and 63MJ per kg of fibre respectively, based on New Zealand Merino Wool Association research[26] (see Figure 5).

Energy use in MJ per kg of fibre

Fibre	MJ per kg
Flax fibre (MAT)	10
Cotton	55
Wool	63
Viscose	100
Polypropylene	115
Polyester	125
Acrylic	175
Nylon	250

*Source: "LCA: New Zealand Merino Wool Total Energy Use", Barber and Pellow, http://www.tech.plym.ac.uk/sme/mats324/mats324A%20ONFETE.htm

Figure 5. Embodied energy used in production of various fibres. Note: MJ is megajoules.

Reconstituted fibres

Viscose (or rayon) is manmade from reconstituted plant fibres and requires 100MJ per kg to produce. Then there's the jump to synthetic fibres made from the non-renewable resources (petroleum, coal or gas) with energy consumption ranging from 115MJ up to 250MJ per kg.

Other manmade fibres derived from plant sources include bamboo, lyocell and modal. They have merit but are produced by a chemical process using potentially hazardous caustic soda (sodium hydroxide) and carbon disulphide. The wood pulp used for lyocell and modal may come from endangered forests, adding further to its environmental burden.[27] New cellulose fibres derived from industrial organic waste are in development and have promise.

While recycled polyester and plastic bottles reincarnated as synthetic (*ie plastic*) fibres may have some social and environmental merit, they are not biodegradable and shed microplastic. Technology for separating and recycling blended fibres (such as poly cottons) is still being refined. Recycled cotton (which has short fibre length) needs to be blended with virgin cotton to be serviceable.

3. Modern-day slavery

Trust in the industrial fashion system was severely dented in 2013. The industry's social licence to operate was shredded when the overcrowded Rana Plaza factory in Bangladesh collapsed, exposing modern-day slavery and the ugly truth of how and where cheap fast fashion is made. On 24 April 2013, 1138 textile workers died, more than 2000 were injured and 800 children orphaned.[28] At the time of the collapse, those workers were shut in an unsafe building, filling an order for fashion companies in developed nations. There can be no excuses for such a lack of safety and duty of care.

That tragic event shone a spotlight for conscientious consumers to turn their purchasing into a force for good by making informed, ethical choices. From it, the global Fashion Revolution movement arose, fostering curiosity, discovery and action towards a fairer fashion future. Fashion Revolution was founded in the United Kingdom and seeks transparency and fairness in the global fashion supply chain, bringing global focus to where and how clothes are made using the hashtag #whomademyclothes. Fashion Revolution has a presence in more than 90 countries including Australia.[29]

To empower Australians and others to purchase from companies that treat workers ethically and reduce the risk of modern slavery, Baptist World Aid Australia has published an Ethical Fashion Report[30] for the past four years. Each report has tracked progress within the industry and indicates significant changes since 2013. The 2017 edition assessed 106 companies, awarding each a grade from A to F based on the strength of their labour rights management systems to mitigate the risk of exploitation in their supply chain.

While this guide is an excellent initiative, the globalised nature of clothing manufacture means a label specifying the country in which a garment is made does not reflect the many different processes and people involved in making clothes. Other resources providing Australian consumer information about ethical options include accreditation group Ethical Clothing Australia[31] and the Good on You app[32], while comparable groups have emerged in other regions.

4. Waste

Fashion automatically comes with perceived obsolescence—the orchestrated creation of dissatisfaction that underpins consumerism.

A continuous stream of new garments are purchased as older garments, no longer considered socially valuable, are shed into the secondhand clothing trade or landfill. Women's fashion garments might be worn only seven times, according to a study by United Kingdom charity Barnardos.[33]

Dressing is an agricultural act,

if we want to wear natural fibres rather than plastic ones.

— Jane Milburn

One of the world's largest fashion brands has acknowledged that too much fashion goes out with the household waste and ends up in landfill. In its Conscious Actions Sustainability Report 2015, fashion retail company H&M wrote:

> Like other industries today, the fashion industry is too dependent on natural resources and we need to change the way fashion is made. This is why we are so committed to our mission to reuse garments and close the loop on textiles. By collecting old clothes and turning them into new updated styles instead of letting them go to waste and by investing in new innovation and technology, we are taking important steps towards a circular economy.[34]

Admirable words yet planned obsolescence and selling more clothes remain at the heart of this business model, where volume and throughput of changing trends drive profit. H&M facilitates consumption through collection bins where old is traded for discount vouchers on new.

Textiles are indeed a fast-growing part of the household waste stream, making up three to five per cent of garbage.[35] In 2013, the Council of Textile and Fashion Industries of Australia[36] warned Australians were sending $500 million of fashion clothing to landfill every year.

According to Australian Bureau of Statistics 2013 figures[37], 500 million kg of leather and textiles are discarded to landfill each year. That equates to 23kg of leather and textiles (including carpets) for every Australian. In the 2017 Australian Broadcasting Corporation series *War on Waste*, Craig Reucassel reported that Australians sent 6000kg of clothing and textiles to landfill every 10 minutes. Similarly, in an earlier series in the United Kingdom, Hugh Fearnley-Whittingstall reported the British discarded 7000kg every 10 minutes.

People discard clothing for many reasons: making way for new; boredom; de-cluttering; dated style; change in body shape; the owner has moved on; garments need mending; or to help a charity.

We are encouraged to donate unwanted clothing—known as post-consumer waste—to charities where items are resold and recycled as an important revenue stream for community work. Donations are then redistributed.[38] About 60 per cent is sold as clothing: 10 per cent locally and 50 per cent to the global trade. A further 15 per cent become industrial rags and 25 per cent goes to landfill.

In Australia, 2500 charitable outlets operate under the umbrella of the National Association of Charitable Recycling Organisations. NACRO reported that Australia exported 70,000 tonnes— or 70 million kg—of secondhand clothing in 2012 sold for an estimated value of about $70 million ($1/kg). By 2016, worn clothing exports increased to 88 million kg,[39] a growth rate of about 25 per cent in four years, reflecting the upward trajectory in new clothing mentioned earlier.

The global secondhand market isn't a long-term solution and is threatening local culture. As *The Economist*[40] reported, South African countries are moving to ban Western cast-offs to protect local industries in the face of the unrelenting secondhand influx. In India, Western clothing is not sold as clothing: rather it is immediately reconstituted into homewares and blankets.[41]

Arguably, the volume of secondhand clothing shipped offshore is Western countries shifting waste to developing nations where it has to be eventually buried or burned (if not shipped back as upcycled homewares!).

Nearly one-third of clothing went into landfill in the UK, according to WRAP in its 2012 *Valuing our clothes* report.[42] It responded with a Love Your Clothes awareness campaign that has achieved positive change[43]—the amount of clothing discarded in residual waste has fallen from 350,000 tonnes (2012) to 300,000 tonnes (2015). Its 2016 report said despite some improvements, the carbon footprint of clothing in use in the UK had risen due to increasing new purchases.[44]

Jane Milburn being interviewed by ABC *War on Waste* crusader Craig Reucassel.

In Queensland, Australia, I addressed a 2015 Brisbane City Council meeting about the need for a more sustainable clothing culture.[45] The council responded in 2016 by initiating Revive, an annual pop-up secondhand fashion festival as a textile waste minimisation strategy—believed to be the first in the world.[46] Additionally, Reverse Garbage Queensland reported that textiles had become its fastest-growing product stream as local businesses diverted excess stock to the warehouse for resale rather than sending it to landfill. Reverse Garbage responded with a Worn OUT?!? Refashion exhibition in 2017 which I co-curated.[47]

5. Loss of knowledge and skills

Few people in Australia sew. Having access or skills to use a sewing machine are relatively rare these days. Home made is sometimes considered old-fashioned as consumers embrace easy (and cheap) opportunities to buy off the rack. The more consumers bought into ready-made, the more we lost the skills and confidence to 'do for ourselves', thereby becoming disempowered and dependent.

Generally speaking, sewing skills, knowledge and understanding have diminished to the point where, across the population, we are now physically dependent and may not even know the basics of mending, let alone making, our clothes. My anecdotal experience is that by the age of 10 years, only about half of schoolchildren have used a needle and thread and many lack the fine-motor skills to do so. In the United Kingdom, the *Daily Mail* has reported that seven out of 10 young people don't know how to sew on a button.[48]

The implications of this may not be immediately obvious because older family members with skills can provide support, or items can be replaced rather than repaired. The dependency and wastefulness of these strategies will become more evident in time.

In *Sustainable fashion and textiles: design journeys*, Fletcher noted the energy used to collect, sort and sell secondhand garments was between 10 and 20 times less than that needed to make a new item; that while repairing and reconditioning garments saved resources compared with manufacturing new items, it required labour and materials. In earlier times the incentive to repair was economic, with techniques such as turning over worn collars and cuffs, patching trousers and shirts, darning holes in socks being accepted practice:

> … within two generations, the financial incentive to repair has largely disappeared, mainly because the price of new garments and textiles has fallen dramatically relative to the cost of labour. Repairing garments at home—if it takes place at all—is now motivated less by economics and more by ethical factors or lifestyle choices like down-shifting and voluntary simplicity.

The teaching of practical life skills such as cooking and sewing has been in decline in schools for three decades. Yet the connection between healthy eating behaviours and teaching children to cook and grow food has been recognised by teachers, health groups, food leaders and governments. The rise of television cooking shows and access to cooking

Stiltwalker wearing Textile Beat upcycled crocheted shorts at REVIVE 2016 event. Photo courtesy of Brisbane City Council.

Jane Milburn with Brisbane City Councillor Peter Matic at Revive 2016.

Textile Beat upcycled garment at Reverse Garbage Queensland 2015 refashion event.

classes outside of school hours provide further opportunities to learn these skills, although more is needed.

Similarly, through the Great British *Sewing Bee*[49], the BBC built a following around home sewing and upcycling. Although the future of that program is in doubt, more community engagement programs like it are needed because people have lost sight of the making process. In an *Examination of apparel maintenance skills and practices: Implications for sustainable clothing consumption*, Pamela Norum discusses the knowledge gap in basic sewing skills among American consumers over time, concluding:

If we believe that consumers need to make changes in their behaviour towards more sustainable clothing consumption, they need the skills to do so.[50]

Industry innovation

There is growing recognition of the need to develop a circular economy, to reduce waste and avoid pollution through regenerative and closed-loop approaches.

Fashion suppliers might achieve sustainability through transparent local design, production and distribution of garments that fosters emotional attachment and longer useable life. New service offerings include renting, leasing or garment exchanges as well as services that upgrade, update, repair or modify products to extend their useful life by delaying psychological obsolescence for consumers.

International examples include the American outdoor clothing company Patagonia offering a repair service and recycle program and the Netherlands-based MUD Jeans pioneering a leasing model for jeans and including 20 per cent recycled cotton in its products.[51] In Australia, Citizen Wolf[52] offers individualised t-shirts with the fabric and style tweaked for a perfect fit. Meanwhile, in an imaginative nod to sustainability, Dutch fashion artists Victor & Rolf repurpose old

Worn OUT?!? 2017 co-curators Jane Milburn and Elizabeth Kingston with model Liyana Jumahat in a Karen Benjamin plastic statement dress 'Solutions'. Photo by Dan Fidler.

garments and materials as a statement about eco-friendly fashion.[53]

All governments are recognising change is needed. *The Guardian* newspaper reported the Swedish government introduced tax breaks on repairs to everything from bicycles, clothes and washing machines in a bid to counter a throwaway culture.[54]

Individual innovation

We can create change through our choices, as we discuss in Chapter 4 and the Slow Clothing Manifesto. In fact the greatest beneficial change would occur if we purchased less clothing and kept it for longer, according to a 2006 UK University of

Jane with MUD Jeans founder Bert von Son at the Sustainable Brands 2016 conference in Sydney.

Cambridge study.[55] Extending the life of clothes by just nine extra months of active use reduces their carbon, water and waste footprints by around 20–30 per cent.[56]

As we have gained by having cheap fast fashion on tap, we have also lost the mindful, creative, resourceful benefits of doing things for ourselves. That's one of the reasons why I undertook a social-change project in 2014 aimed at shifting thinking about the way clothing and textiles were consumed. The 365-day Sew it Again[57] project demonstrated creative ways to upcycle clothing and empower individuals to tap into the 'greenest' clothing of all, that already existing in wardrobes and op shops. It highlighted the value of sewing skills, encouraged a culture of thrift, and showed heartfelt concern. This was followed in 2016 by The Slow Clothing Project engaging like-minded makers across Australia. Chapter 3 highlights these projects.

For some, choosing to sew was seen as a betrayal of feminism. While I grew up knowing how, I didn't often admit to what seemed a domestic rather than a feminist skill. Author and activist Tara Moss chose to associate with traditionally masculine endeavours, like motorbike riding, in the 1990s rather than 'feminised' skills. She is now learning to mend and sew, recognising the usefulness, self-sufficiency and creativity of these skills.[58]

Author Judi Kettler in *Sew Retro: a stylish history of the sewing revolution* acknowledged sewing skills for women went out, along with corsets and long hair, when their right to vote came in. She said with third-wave feminism, sewing is making a comeback. Now we sew for empowerment, creativity and sustainability.

Until recently, the thought of 'making do' as stoic Brits and others did during tough times was stigmatised. Repair was interpreted as poverty or thrift, in a world readily accepting waste in pursuit of everyday perfection. We are now recalibrating that, with visible mending being seen as a confident, creative statement about sustainable values, rather than impoverishment.

The Repair Café, initiated in Amsterdam by Martine Postma, is a case in point, becoming a global movement of free meeting places where

people interested in repairing things or giving them a new lease of life come together.

And so to Slow Clothing

What we wear impacts planetary health in ways that we are only beginning to understand. We endure marketing that attempts to convince us we need more to be fulfilled. Yet in the rush to own things for reasons of status and looks, we lose the opportunity to be mindful, resourceful and creative. Until we make something for ourselves to wear, we cannot fully appreciate the resources, time and skills that go into the clothes we buy.

We *can* step off the treadmill of constant and conspicuous consumption. People with a few hand-stitching skills can enjoy the independence of being able to make, upcycle, mend and adapt their garments. We can gain a sense of achievement and emotional attachment to our original work, while wearing garments that flatter our own body shape. Financial, social and psychological benefits flow from making sustainable and ethical clothing choices. Perhaps most importantly, we know no-one was exploited in the process.

In *This changes everything*, Naomi Klein says all living things must take from nature to survive but that this should be done responsibly, with caretaking and a commitment to renewal and regeneration.

Living nonextractively means relying overwhelmingly on resources that can be continuously regenerated: deriving our food from farming methods that protect soil fertility; our energy from methods that harness the ever-renewing strength of the sun, wind and waves; our metals from recycled and reused sources.

And what of our clothes? Klein's words speak to me of a return to localisation. We have done globalisation; it works for those who control the power and money. Cheap clothes in big fashion stores arrive on the back of exploitation of resources and people in places unseen and offshore. With a return to localism, there is potential to care, share and create a better ecosystem. We nurture local production when we are prepared to pay a little more for products. We need to value low clothing miles, as we do low food miles. Shifts in thinking are becoming more visible as individuals seek to live more sustainably, as conscious dressers seek to know more about the substance of what we wear, not just the style or the cut.

With the global population at 7.5 billion and more people living in cities rather than rural and regional areas, we have moved through the Agricultural Age, the Industrial Age and the Information Age. We are now in the Conceptual Age, as outlined in Daniel Pink's book *A whole new mind*, when empathy, stories and meaning-making are rising qualities. Surely clothes that mean something to us personally, that carry a good story about how they came to be in the world are much more likely to last in our wardrobes than flash and crash fashion?

In *Sustainable fashion and textiles: design journeys*, Fletcher argued most of us have a fairly lifeless and disappointing relationship with our clothes:

> This lack of engagement starts as we go shopping for clothes and continues as we wear these garments … products on sale on the high street are becoming homogenous and this lack of choice erodes our individuality and dulls our imagination, limiting our confidence about what clothes can be.

It is assumed we, the wearers, will follow prescribed trends and accept being increasingly distanced from the creative process. Fletcher said:

> Ready-made garments appear to offer us the promise of something better than we could make ourselves. Although when we go down the route of buying into this perceived perfection, we end up forgoing an opportunity to learn how to make things and become more skilled. As deskilled individuals, we play into the hands of consumerist fashion.

This is what Slow Clothing is about. We are not passive. We reclaim our power to make choices for ourselves. We resist the fashion system's influence by asserting our individuality, originality and creativity. We are reskilling, gaining confidence to dress in individual style rather than in a shadow determined and limited by others. We want to live in a sustainable world that does not waste or exploit resources and people. Slow Clothing is a pathway to living simply and fairly, by dressing creatively and authentically.

Sewing and stitching are life skills, just like cooking and baking.
Life skills enable us to provide for ourselves.

— Jane Milburn

Jane Milburn wearing her history skirt at the Burdekin River in north Queensland. Photo by Fiona Lake.

Chapter 2

AUTHENTICITY

My journey to Slow Clothing
Agricultural science, rural communications, natural-fibre champion

Precisely when my Slow Clothing journey began is hard to pin down because the fabric of life meanders.

We all spring from somewhere then navigate our way, gathering intelligence from immersion in the doing. Looking back, the pathway I chose was organic and fluid. Yet it is intriguing to now see how those threads of learning, early work in journalism, communications and advocacy—as well as parenting and evolving as a human being—led to this purposeful work of finding meaning in what we wear.

Natural fibres and connection to garments made by me, for me, have always been me.

That spun into something more when I began following my heart on a creative journey in 2012. I discovered new meaning in upcycling (clothes and life experiences!) that reconnected to my past and helped weave a different future.

This is the story of my mended and upcycled life.

So when did the upcycling begin?

It could have been in 2012 when I drove from Brisbane to Townsville and back, stopping at every charity shop (op shop) that was open. Yes, flying would have been quicker, easier and cheaper but I chose the slow way, the 2700km journey giving me plenty of time for reflection. I had been forced to resign from my job, leadership concept shredded. My youngest child had just finished school: main parenting role was nearly over. For the second time in my life, on doctor's advice, I was taking anti-depressants (something I hated!). I travelled alone, overnighting with friends, gathering treasure with each stop. *A clear lesson from that trip: there are many resources available all around us, when we stop to look.*

Perhaps the Slow Clothing journey began a year earlier, when I rediscovered op shopping after attending a pre-loved fashion fundraising event. A bid in the silent auction secured me Australian TV personality Kerri-Anne Kennerley's leather jacket for $75. Bargain! I bought a brown and white houndstooth jacket for $14 because I love chocolate brown. Towards night's end, the price dropped to $2 per item and I selected 30 perfectly good tops for $60. I refashioned them and other finds into office wear for the day job. *Lesson learned: clothing has become so plentiful and affordable we are virtually giving it away.*

Track back to 2009, when I bought a magnificent cashmere Birger Christensen coat for $120 at a preloved store in Toronto for extra warmth while visiting my son Casey who was studying at McGill University in Montreal, Canada. Nothing like an overseas trip to appreciate that a suitcase of clothing is enough. I remember seeing a 'Fur is Green' advertisement and thinking it was clever marketing to position fur as a natural, renewable and recyclable resource. Fake fur is plastic. *Lesson learned: So many beautiful garments exist in the world. Do we need to buy new?*

Or did the Slow Clothing journey begin back to the 1990s when I developed my own creativity by playing with fabric paint, textiles and three little children? With two toddlers Casey and Max, we moved from Townsville to Brisbane for my partner Darcy's work as an exploration geologist and I worked part-time as a sub-editor at *The Courier-Mail* newspaper. Home on maternity leave with Lily, our third, I went on a sewing bender in my bolt-hole of a studio and made an entire wardrobe of garments for myself after discovering a source of gorgeous yet affordable linen and knits. *Lesson learned: Making clothes to suit oneself is satisfying.*

Perhaps it began before children, in the 1980s when my aunt Kate McLachlan taught me to spin wool from the fleece of her black and coloured sheep that I knitted into a jumper for Darcy and a long sleeveless vest for myself. *Lesson learned: Slow skills enables the making of uniquely personal garments.*

Earlier still, it might have begun in the late 1970s when I was at university studying agricultural science with an eclectic wardrobe of handmade and thrifted finds—as well as two rayon dresses gifted from my great aunt that I restyled by taking in and up. I had a reputation as a fashion queen among my fellow aggies, who were more likely to be wearing country gear of checked shirts and denim jeans with RM Williams boots. *Lesson learned: Clothes enable us to show individuality.*

Or did it start when I made my first dress at age 13, a simple blue floral cotton shift with the shortest of hemlines, and pink striped curtains for my bedroom window? *Lesson learned: Sewing was once a life skill learned at school.*

Simplicity of childhood

Grounded in homespun references to earlier and simpler times, I see there are many threads stitched into my Slow Clothing philosophy that has been a lifetime in the making.

The first decade of my life was spent on a sheep farm near Owaka in Otago on the South Island of New Zealand. I have fond memories of making daisy chains, picking fruit and climbing the hills for picnics in summer; of the wood stove, bare trees and cracking the icy puddles as we waited in the shelter for the school bus in winter.

Mum, Dad and four siblings lived in the big house on the farm at Hunt Road while our (Great) Grandma Mary lived in a wooden cottage. We had a lot to do with Grandma growing up—she taught us to 'do what you do, do well'. While Dad worked the farm, Mum was a teacher. It was Grandma who often cooked our main meal of the day—using home-butchered meat and vegetables from the kitchen garden. Grandma was already into her 80s and I remember the occasional earwig in the spinach that escaped her notice! Such oversights aside, we learned life skills from her and only later understood that she was connected back to hunter-gatherer ancestors as a daughter of Maori (Ngāi Tahu) and Scottish parents. Great Grandma survived well into her 101st year, enjoying a simple life down on the farm. Our school holidays were filled with opportunities to learn to knit, crochet, bake, cook, make preserves, grow vegetables, pick cherries and walnuts, and forage for mushrooms after rain, sometimes with Mum's mother, our Nana Garth.

In this environment, fruit, vegetables and meat were largely home-grown or locally sourced. Natural resources such as wool, wood and water were valued and used in accordance with the 'waste not, want not' philosophy which was the norm for generations past. Only later in life, reflecting back on these times before consumption and consumer-culture became the dominant order, did

I appreciate the intrinsic value of self-sufficiency and skills for sustainable living.

Mum was university educated and a home economics teacher, and it was always assumed that we too would go to university. It was from Mum that I gained an enduring interest in making my own clothes. She sewed almost everything we wore

Wearing their Sunday Best outfits made by Mum, siblings Joanne, Tony and (Lindy) Jane with Dad.

The Capon children: Tony, (Lindy) Jane, Paul and Joanne wearing sailor suits made by their Mum, circa 1965.

in those early years—often matching sets for all four children like shades of the von Trapp family in *The Sound of Music*!

Farm life is idyllic through the eyes of a child but for education and future opportunities, Mum and Dad moved our family to south-east Queensland, Australia, where I spent the second decade of life. Although a simple migrant experience, this border-crossing, and the early death of Mum, was to shape the way I would interact with the world.

Thrift and resourcefulness were family hallmarks. Look after the pennies and the pounds will take care of themselves. As an example of how this played, we did belt-tightening at one stage to pay an unexpected provisional tax bill. Breakfast cereal was on special, with a limit of two packets per person. Dad and the four children were dispatched to the shops, and one by one with required cash in hand we moved through the checkout. Although perfectly legitimate, as the last of the siblings, I remember our strategy being noted by a snide remark from the checkout operator. Not to suggest we lived on Weetbix! Every Friday morning, as regular as clockwork, Dad went to Rocklea wholesale markets to buy cartons of seasonal fruit and vegetables. It was my job to restock the fridge. *Save where you can, to achieve what you want.*

Another of my tasks was to iron the school shirts on Sunday evening. Maybe that is why I almost never iron anything now! We mostly lived in Brisbane yet stayed connected to our rural roots at a beef cattle farm at Amamoor in the Mary Valley, about 160km north of Brisbane. Our weekend visits, observing nature along the creek and seeing natural farm systems at work, sowed the seeds for my tertiary studies. I completed a Bachelor of Agricultural Science at The University of Queensland in 1979. *Childhood experiences influence choices. Our memories make us who we are.*

While my siblings and I were studying, Mum (Elizabeth Capon) co-authored what was to be a defining home economics textbook with Margaret Rains. First published in 1974, *Focus on Living*[59] encapsulated life skills in a simple and graphic way and was used as a high school resource for more than two decades at a time when the teaching of

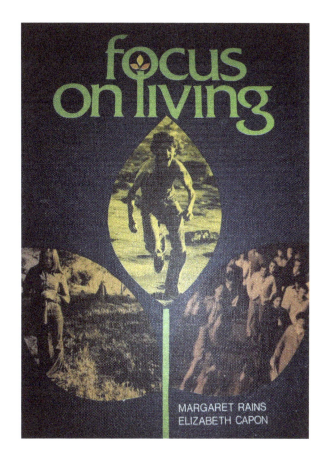

Secondary school text book *Focus on living* co-authored by Mum, Elizabeth Capon.

sustainable skills like cooking and sewing, learning about family relationships and making consumer decisions were all part of the curriculum. *Skills for living are shared across generations and through education.*

Early career experience

The threads of my enduring attachment to natural fibres continued into early career jobs. The first was as a research assistant in 1980 when I did face-to-face interviews with cotton growers in Queensland to gauge their level of knowledge and use of Integrated Pest Management. Although most were aware of IPM, they were still using multiple applications of what was then regarded as a 'safe' chemical, endosulfan, to control heliothis moth. Farm practices have changed dramatically since, with a combination of gene technology and beneficial insects enabling growers to produce sustainable cotton under programs such as the Better Cotton Initiative. *All agricultural production processes have some environmental impact.*

As a rural reporter with the Australian Broadcasting Corporation, my first posting in 1981 was with 3WV/WL Horsham, covering the western half of Victoria. It involved a morning rural report and contributions statewide to *The Country Hour*. This diverse agricultural region created fabulous memories of travelling the countryside, gathering stories about food and fibre production—including fine wool grown in the western districts. The winters were cold so I bought a wool coat in an op shop for a field day where I interviewed then wool industry leader Hugh Beggs, brother-in-law to former prime minister Malcolm Fraser. The rental house I shared had no garage, so the morning frost on the car windscreen had to be coaxed off with water to get to the studio by 5.30am. Because of the early start, breakfast announcer Bernard had a

running on-air joke about me being in a dressing gown and gumboots. Eventually one morning I decided to wear a dressing gown—a modest cotton chenille number—and inexplicably the curious policeman on patrol called into the studio. His eyes popped to see the chat was true. We had chooks in our backyard, and that became safer territory for morning banter with Bernard. In those days of ABC Rural, it was all hands on deck in the big smoke for the flagship annual Melbourne Show Week. When I was required to present the television weather (then a rural responsibility), the most photogenic garment I wore turned out to be a simple hand-knitted jumper in dark forest green that was knitted by Nana Garth. The yellow flounced shirt I purchased was definitely over the top. *The clothes we wear influence the image we project, doubly so in the media.*

Life in the tropics

My next posting was at the other end of Australia, in Townsville, north Queensland, in a television role that included the weather and stories for a statewide rural program. Through work, I met newspaper veteran John Andersen and his wife Robyn from Robin Hood Station, and joined a fun weekend bus trip to Forsayth in the southern Gulf of Carpentaria for the annual rodeo in 1984. I stepped off the bus and met Darcy Milburn who was then working with gold prospecting group,

Clockwise from top-left on opposite page: Jane Milburn presenting ABC TV weather; with Darcy Milburn at Mingella Races; interviewing a goat producer; at ABC Horsham in Victoria; first bush camp erected by Jane near Lakeland in far north Queensland.

Queensland Metals. We've been together since and Darcy has been my champion through all the ups and downs of life.

I left the ABC and went freelancing with Darcy on a drilling job he was overseeing on Cape York Peninsula that involved two months camping on Bromley Station, east of Moreton Telegraph Station. Occasionally the rig broke down and we went beachcombing. This was my first encounter with plastic pollution washed up on remote beaches from the shipping lane. After an interview over the Royal Flying Doctor Radio Service, I started work at the *Townsville Bulletin* newspaper

in 1985 as a reporter and sub-editor. Living in the tropics—and having two babies there—meant wearing simple clothes of cotton and linen that were easy to wash and wear. *Love crush on linen, one of the most environmentally friendly fibres of all.*

Gathering skills

Sometime after we moved to Brisbane, the natural fibres bobbed up again when I worked as a media advisor for then Queensland Minister for Primary Industries Henry Palaszczuk. The new millennium had arrived. Amidst more serious responsibilities,

Jane Milburn with Benny Banana and Mad Dog at a north Queensland Cowboys football match in 2004 to raise awareness about the pest and disease risks associated with banana imports. Photo by Chrissy Maguire.

Jane Milburn with country music legend Lee Kernaghan, left, who was part of the AgForce Every Family Needs a Farmer campaign, and, above, with then Water Minister now Australian Prime Minister Malcolm Turnbull at a Rural Press Club lunch she organised as 2007 president. Jane wore the same silk ensemble (made by her) on both occasions. Photo above by Col Jackson.

the minister hosted a Wear Wool Wednesday event in the Red Chamber of the Queensland Parliament featuring gorgeous garments by Australian fashion designer Liz Davenport. Political staff jobs are never easy, particularly when you are not a member of a political party. That job ended for me in challenging circumstances, although the minister and I remain friends. I left with excellent references and returned to the natural fibres—this time as a form of art therapy. For the first time in my life, I needed anti-depressants and counselling. I turned to textiles and threads for soothing and undemanding reassurance as I worked to extend my style from

craft to art. *Playing with natural fibres is mindful art therapy. Take the learning and move forward.*

This was the springboard for my rural media consultancy, Milburn Media and Marketing. One of my clients was the Australian Banana Growers' Council and during the years of 2002-2009, when the Australian industry was threatened with Philippine imports, I worked on the Save the Aussie Banana campaign. Australia is the only Western country that grows its own bananas, and the industry was determined it would not be put at risk from imported pests and diseases. The campaign involved a four-pronged approach of legal, science, political and public awareness. Such integrated work was a great way to engage my political experience, as well as science and journalism. *Previous advocacy work informs the Slow Clothing work I now do.*

Amid this, I wrote freelance stories for *OUTBACK* magazine and *The Courier-Mail*, winning a rural journalism award for a feature about the controversial sale of one of Australia's largest cattle businesses, Stanbroke Pastoral Company. I was also active for eight years with the Rural Press Club, including as president between 2005-2008, helping build its systems, networks and governance to become a respected rural and agribusiness forum.

The natural fibre link continued with other clients—the Leading Sheep project, an industry-government collaboration to rebuild the Queensland sheep industry, and with rural advocacy group AgForce Queensland and its Every Family Needs a Farmer campaign. *Knowledge of natural fibre production in Australia is useful for a natural-fibre champion.*

Gaining self-awareness

While this work was enjoyable and meaningful, the leap to authenticity began with self-awareness gained through the Australian Rural Leadership Program. ARLP provides selected individuals with personal and professional development over 60 days across six immersion trips that included the Kimberley region of Western Australia, Alice Springs in the Northern Territory and India. My

Jane with rural women in India during an ARLP study tour. Photo by Caroline Rhodes.

participation was made possible by the Fairfax Agricultural Media scholarship and I am deeply grateful for the learning and insights it provided. This experience shaped who I am today.

Across an 18-month period of 2009-2010, I learned many things and met many people. One was Keelen Mailman, from Mt Tabor Station at Augathella, the first Aboriginal woman to manage a cattle property in Australia and author of *The Power of Bones*. As our leadership was tested in the Kimberley, Keelen's advice was always straightforward and simple: 'Just follow your heart Jane'. Another learning, gained from the bottom of a dry gully, came by way of a quote shared by our colleague Anthony Shelly 'Leadership is an action you take, not a position you hold'.[60] *You don't need a title or a badge to be a leader, you can just step up.*

Jane Milburn with Australian Rural Leadership Program colleagues in the Kimberley region of Western Australia, from left, Anthony Shelly, Mike Mooney, Keelen Mailman, Dallas King and Andrew Mencshelyi. Jane wears linen garments made for herself. Photo by Russell Fisher.

I took the opportunity to pitch a social media project about sharing stories of sustainable food production in Australia through a digital platform, Food Farming Australia.[61] With interest in food and television cooking shows rising, there was a need to connect consumers with where and how their food was grown. The project was 2010 Queensland runner-up in the Rural Women's Award and the headline was *Who grew my dinner?* While no funding came with the runner-up title, it propelled me to learn blogging and social media skills which I pocketed for later use when I turned my attention from the food story to the clothing story.

Creating change

Late 2010, saw me step into a role as communications manager for preventive health group Diabetes Queensland. This was a move to the health side of food, complementing earlier work on the farming side of food. I had skills, knowledge, experience, ideas and contacts to contribute. Personally it also became an opportunity to focus on my own health, as I realised my waist measurement put me at risk of type 2 diabetes. When 2011 rolled around with a trim svelte self, thanks to a diet of protein and vegetables, this coincided with the rediscovery of preloved clothing mentioned earlier. For relaxation, I began seeking out and rescuing natural-fibre garments such as wool jumpers with holes or linen shirts with missing buttons. Although I did not realise it at the time, as I fixed and refashioned these finds into office wear, the seeds for my next career incarnation were being sown. *Nothing you learn is ever wasted.*

Jane (wearing upcycled silk) with then Queensland Minister for Health Lawrence Springborg. Photo by Patria Jannides.

As part of this day job, we had secured federal government funding to work collaboratively with other non-government health organisations on a healthy weight project. An ambitious leadership concept popped into my head one night. I had almost a decade of experience with the Rural Press Club and was part of a core group that reactivated it into a thriving network for agribusiness and the bush. The Swap It project presented an opportunity to create an equivalent health network to raise awareness of the range of preventable health conditions caused by the growing societal problem of obesity. I proposed the Health Media Club as a vehicle to bring health groups together to canvass issues important to a society and health budget weighed down by lifestyle-induced conditions. Being action-oriented, I set about developing a framework for the club and involved three health journalists as part of an advisory committee. We ran two successful events on my watch—the first with the Minister for Health Lawrence Springborg[62] and the second with public health academic and plain-packaging on tobacco campaigner Professor Mike Daube. Two other events were in the pipeline.

From my experience with the Rural Press Club, I knew the Health Media Club needed to be run independently if we were to keep the faith of journalists, other groups and interested parties. While it was initiated under the auspices of the organisation I was employed by, I had proposed that it needed to be established independently and run by a cross-sector committee. My position became untenable when I discovered, through an ASIC search, that my employer had itself registered

Jane Milburn (wearing upcycled silk top and wool skirt) with ABC presenter Tim Cox. Photo by Patria Jannides.

the Health Media Club before the first event had been run. I left that job and the Health Media Club withered on the vine. *Positional roles are not where transformation happens.*

Digging for treasure

That journey brings me to the long slow road trip in 2012, reflecting on what I had learned in life and what was next. I didn't stay depressed long. While in Townsville, north Queensland, with friends Chrissy Maguire and Peter Buckle, I met the amazingly creative Mary Ede of The Skirt. In her beautiful studio, Mary demonstrated the magic of clothes and inspired me to create my first History Skirt when I returned to Brisbane. On the homeward journey, stopping in the Burdekin sugarcane town of Ayr at another op shop, I remembered an old tea box I had carried around for years, full of cotton lace offcuts from garments that Mum had made me and my sister. These were tangible memories of childhood, of Mum, of an earlier life. Unless I used them in a productive, creative way, they would be cast aside when I was no longer around…

As I turned into the driveway of my Brisbane home, Honda Civic hybrid full of thrifted nature-fibre treasures, I knew where my future lay. *Follow your heart to live your values.*

Within weeks, before 2012 was farewelled, I had created my first History Skirt: a gored skirt with two panels made of lace offcuts from my earlier life, and another six pieced together from op shop linen and silk garments gathered on the trip. To me, this

encapsulated natural fibres and their place in our clothing story. The skirt features on the cover of this book.

By this stage, Lily had finished Year 12 and both Max and Casey were graduates, employed, partnered-up and soon to move out of home. The pressure was off, parenting job nearly done, empty nest imminent. In 2013, I completed a Graduate Certificate of Australian Rural Leadership through James Cook University alongside textile immersion in a studio that expanded to fill the physical and emotional space left by departing children. In this year too, my youngest brother Paul died suddenly while working in Western Australia. This was cause for sadness and more reflection about what makes a meaningful life.

It was valuable to undertake postgrad study that was grounded in my own life and leadership experience. One subject provided an opportunity to reflect on my experience with the Health Media Club. I came to understand the difference between positional and transformational leadership. Seeking to work innovatively and collaboratively for the greater good, was seen as a risk to the status quo. A second subject provided the opportunity to research textile waste and develop my new social enterprise business, Textile Beat.

Threads of change

My anecdotal op-shopping research had indicated a growing mountain of clothing excess. The potential waste of resources troubled me, as did my

Jane in Kuala Lumpur in 2013 with brother Tony Capon, then director of UN University's International Institute for Global Health.

observation that these clothes were predominantly synthetic fibres rather than natural ones. *Synthetic fibres are plastic, derived from petroleum.*

I wondered about the overarching changes in the way we dress brought on by globalisation providing increasingly cheap clothing options. When I searched for it back in early 2013, there was little information or awareness about textile waste and the environmental impact of our clothing. Few were thinking this way in Australia at that time.

Journalists Lucy Siegle in the United Kingdom and Elizabeth Cline in the United States had published books while in Hong Kong, Christina Dean had set up Redress after observing clothing becoming landfill. In Australia, fashion writer Clare Press published *Wardrobe Crisis: How we went from Sunday best to fast fashion* in 2016.

The fashion world changed irrevocably with the Bangladesh Rana Plaza factory collapse in 2013. As images beamed into homes on the TV news, I knew my future was grounded in the antithesis of this cheap, exploitative fashion. I resolved to show another way that did not buy into the always-new consumption treadmill.

That year Textile Beat began raising awareness of the role clothing plays in our lives to inspire more sustainable and ethical approaches to dressing rather than fast fashion, and to help ameliorate the growing problem of clothing waste. I knew the narrative that existed around food was needed for clothing: that the conversation needed to change from being dominated by style, fashion, brand and price to being more about the substance, origins, longevity and making of our clothes. The first blog post in July 2013 was: Creative ways to cherish and value natural fibres

> In a finite world, we need to treasure our limited natural resources and beautiful things made from fibres, wood, leather, stone and shells. Instead of tossing them away when they have fallen out of favour, we are exploring creative ways to repurpose them for a second life.

I did not have a strategic plan and instead my Slow Clothing philosophy evolved organically, through the doing. My brother, Professor Tony Capon from The University of Sydney, tells me I am providing leadership, capacity building and engagement in the everyday practice of what we wear.

From my perspective, I am also following my heart on a creative journey which brings together all that I am. This work connects my family history and childhood experiences, and taps into my love of natural fibres and the therapeutic and creative power of making. It utilises my education and professional experience, and desire to work to my values of authenticity, creativity, autonomy and purpose.

In his book *A New Earth: awakening to your life's purpose,* Eckhart Tolle said that when you are authentic and don't play roles, it means there is no self (ego) in what you do. When there is no secondary agenda to protect or strengthen yourself, then your actions have far greater power—and therefore capacity to influence and create positive change. Tolle wrote:

> In a world of role-playing personalities, those few people who don't project a mind-made image but function from the deeper core of their being, those who do not attempt to appear more than they are but are simply themselves, stand out as remarkable and are the only ones who truly make a difference in this world.

Values-based living

I am a pragmatic and practical person, as is my story. I had no problem in refashioning preloved natural-fibre clothes and making things: that's being true to my values. (I do buy new underwear and shoes.)

Textile Beat's first project was a year-long challenge called Sew It Again. It involved bringing new life to a rescued garment on a daily basis during 2014 and, through its blog, exploring and documenting upcycling options and clothing issues. Sew It Again (Chapter 3) was a platform for speaking out about the need for a more sustainable clothing culture.

In 2015, I developed the Slow Clothing Manifesto as an overarching framework to reduce our material footprint by acting thoughtfully in the way we buy, use and discard our clothing. The manifesto (Chapter 4) includes 10 actions: think, natural, quality, local, few, care, make, revive, adapt and salvage.

In 2016, The Slow Clothing Project documented 40 Australians who choose to sew garments for themselves to wear, again showcasing handmade approaches to help advance the ethics and sustainability of our clothing story. Some of their stories are captured in Chapter 3.

Both Sew It Again and The Slow Clothing Project were based on an ethos of self-sufficiency: anything old can be new again when we have the skills and willingness to invest time in it. What has troubled me throughout this journey has been

Jane Milburn runs a regular Clothing Repair Cafe at Reverse Garbage Queensland.

the loss of skills to enable individuals to 'buy into' Slow Clothing: not knowing how to thread a needle, hand stitch, use a sewing machine, darn a hole in a garment. This has led to my involvement in upcycling and repair workshops, giving others the inspiration and some capacity to be creative, sustainable, individual dressers.

Other actions

Through Textile Beat, I have been invited to present hundreds of talks and workshops across Australia. I share what I have learned about clothing, sustainability and living simply. I also regularly host a Clothing Repair Cafe at Reverse Garbage Queensland and continue to learn from the people I meet. Following a chance encounter with Japanese textile artist Akiko Ike[63] in Brisbane, I travelled to Niigata in Japan to learn about boro, sashiko and chiku chiku stitching. While there, I was also introduced to weaving in Osaka with Misao and Kenzo Jo at Saorinomori. Misao believes the spirit of weaving exists in the spirit of living a life freely and faithfully to your true self, apart from conventional ways. In her book, *SAORI: Self-innovation through free weaving*, Misao said:

Jane met Akiko Ike at a Brisbane craft event.

Jane met 103-year-old Misao Jo at Saorinomori in Osaka, Japan. Photo by Kenzo Jo.

It is superficial just to put on the clothing that you purchased at a store. Genuine fashion expresses our true selves just as our faces do.

We create our own patterns based on our lives and we should wear them. The other valuable insight I learned from this book is the concept of self-innovation: being the best you can be, which involves making changes and taking risks.

Personal expression

A rural colleague recently mentioned the concept of expressing personality through clothing choices and perceived, correctly, that I am INFP on the Myers-Briggs personality test. The Truity website[64] defines INFP-character traits as:

- **Introverted**
  Composed, self-reliant, reserved and thoughtful

- **Intuitive**
  Creative, imaginative, idealistic and innovative

- **Feeling**
  Empathetic, sensitive, ethical and authentic

- **Perceiving**
  Flexible, accepting, tolerant and open-minded

Jane's former boss Henry Palaszczuk at a Textile Beat four-year milestone event. Photo by Patria Jannides.

Truity says INFPs are imaginative idealists, guided by their own core values and beliefs. They see potential for a better future, and pursue truth and meaning with their own individual flair. Individualistic and non-judgmental, INFPs enjoy spending time exploring their own ideas and values, are creative and often artistic; they enjoy finding new outlets for self-expression. INFPs value authenticity and want to be original and individual in what they do. They are often concerned with a search for meaning and truth within themselves. Following tradition holds little appeal for the INFP; they prefer to do their own exploration of values and ideas, and decide for themselves what seems right. INFPs are often offbeat and unconventional, but they feel no desire to conform. The INFP would rather be true to themselves than try to fit in with the crowd. The INFP may react strongly if they feel their own values are being violated, and they want an open, supportive exchange of ideas. INFPs engage themselves in a lifelong quest for meaning and authenticity. *Personality type explains a lot.*

Well that's it then. These insights into my personality type explain so much—in hindsight—about this Slow Clothing journey. It is useful to explore personality type to gain perspective on how we want to live. We are all on a different journey. Through this narrative, I am making sense of mine.

We all have the capacity to change, contribute and choose our own pathways. Often it is the small decisions we make every day that can have major influence on our lifestyle, lifespan and life choices.

The potted history just shared outlines how I came to be where I am today, yet there are other experiences and observations that were pivotal—and three I want to specifically mention.

Critical insights

We know the resources on Earth are finite, yet sometimes we consume them as if they were not. Although it is no longer top-of-mind for many, the urban water crisis in my city of Brisbane a decade ago continues to inform the way I live today.

Brisbane, in the Australian state of Queensland, was gripped by a statewide drought in 2006 to the point where severe domestic water-use restrictions were introduced across the south-east. Television images of Brisbane city's main water supply of Wivenhoe

Dam heading below 17% capacity alarmed us all. Consumption was limited to 140 litres per person per day. Chronic overusers faced heavy fines; their shower pressure was reduced to a trickle. Incredible community-wide behaviour change in reducing household water consumption was achieved because people understood the impact of their actions. We became conscious of water and made different decisions for a while, because our survival depended on our actions. For me, it brought back memories of Grandma and Nana being careful with water on the farm, capturing any kitchen surplus to water herbs near the back door. We, like many others, had buckets in our shower to capture surplus before the water ran hot which we then poured on the garden. We installed two rainwater tanks to conserve water for a non-rainy day.

Although the crisis receded as rain arrived and infrastructure was improved, the legacy of that time for me was greater awareness that Nature's bounty is finite. In our home to this day, we are careful with water by washing clothes less, having shorter showers and gardening with less-needy plants. *When we understand the environmental impact, we can change our choices and behaviours.*

Another story pertains to the use of reclaimed resources when extending our living space in 2004 as our three children became teenagers. While the builder was sympathetic to our sustainable values and desire to reuse and upcycle existing materials, he gave good arguments for importing new materials rather than expending time and energy restoring, reshaping and retrofitting. Time is money. It often costs more to reuse and upcycle resources. This disconnect between price and value is a dilemma that permeates every aspect of our lives, and helps explain why Australia's waste burden is growing at a annual compounding rate of 7.8 per cent.[65] While we had to concede on some aspects, we stayed true to our values with others. Today we still enjoy the gorgeous Crows Ash floorboards salvaged from an old squash court as our living room floor. *Being sustainable may cost more, but it is worth it in the long run.*

My final story is a personal one about how small individual decisions have the potential to impact our health and lifespan. Mum died in 1980 from bowel cancer that was diagnosed too late. Losing a parent creates a hole that is never filled. I was

Jane Milburn presented a TEDxQUT talk in 2017, Slow Clothing in a material world.

22 and just out of university. Life had to go on, yet looking back now I see the grief was papered over with career ambition and soothed with alcohol.

Nana went some way to being a replacement mum, although more in a caring than in a career-mentoring sense. Then in 1993, Nana too died from cancer—this time lung cancer, even though she never smoked, drank little alcohol and lived a simple life down on the farm where we grew up.

These losses, and the pattern of cancer in the genes, strengthened my commitment to eat healthily and be physically active, yet alcohol was omnipresent. I gave it up for an entire year in 2004 to set a good example for our teenage boys. Can't be saying one thing ('be careful with drink and drugs') while doing another. Yet after that year of abstinence, I gradually returned to the old habits of too much red wine at night. Drinking alcohol, sometimes to excess, is an accepted Australian societal norm. Back in the day, it was considered a tool of trade for aggies and journalists. It easily becomes an every night thing. I guess I was what people refer to as a functioning alcoholic and I thought it helped me be creative.

It wasn't until I was diagnosed with early stage breast cancer for which I had surgery and radiotherapy in 2007 that I noticed, and read, numerous studies about the connection between cancer and regular drinking. I kept working throughout the treatment and chose to accept the imperfection of one breast being smaller and wonkier rather than have reconstruction surgery. It is a reminder that nothing in life is perfect. *Embrace imperfection, trying to be perfect is impossible to maintain.*

I also heeded the warning and have lived alcohol-free since 2009. Darcy still enjoys his red and I missed it for a while. Now I love that I can always drive and never have hangovers. I also love the calmness and clarity of thought. I try to keep my weight within the healthy range, eating mostly vegetables and some protein.

Neither weight-loss nor living alcohol-free are easy in a culture drenched with alcohol and unhealthy food temptations. We have everything to excess, including possessions and clothes. *Our choices influence our outcomes.*

A process for finding authenticity

- **take time** – to reflect on what you value most

- **be enough** – stop striving to be more or have more

- **seek allies** – find people and networks that resonate

- **keep learning** – find ways to grow through play

- **choose health** – make wellbeing a daily priority

- **respect process** – a plan helps set your sails

- **follow your heart** – be true to yourself

Abundantly clear

It is only in the past 100 years or so that abundance has created high-consumption lifestyles with a multitude of contrived and perceived needs that foster feelings of dissatisfaction with the status quo.

If we reflect on our intangible health needs as outlined in Stephen Boyden's *The Biology of Civilisation*, we understand that including opportunities for creative behaviour and learning manual skills are important for our wellbeing. They bring a sense of personal involvement and purpose. This is worth remembering at a time when many of our needs are ready-made for us to just consume.

I am grateful to have found a way to meet these intangible needs through upcycling and this Slow Clothing work, wrapped up in love and care for family, friendships and the natural world. This brings meaning and purpose to my life.

Just as reconnecting to the source of our food, learning to grow and cook can help us make healthier eating choices, so can an understanding of how clothes are made and learning mending skills empower us to make 'healthier' clothing choices.

Jane Milburn sharing creative upcycling ideas at a Textile Beat library workshop.

Embrace imperfection.
Being perfect is impossible to maintain.

— Jane Milburn

- -

Living sustainably, based on the principles of permaculture and sufficiency, incorporates knowing how to grow and cook—AND—make and mend. I know this because I live it. I write this book as a new grandmother, in the hope that my grandchildren and their children's children can continue to live well into the future. A homespun philosophy of valuing the old may be at odds with contemporary culture of forever more new, yet I pursue it in the belief that a circular approach will eventually bring these two perspectives together.

This book—and the work that I now do—is a sum of the many parts of my life and career upcycled. I am living and wearing my values of authenticity, creativity, autonomy and purpose. It brings my Slow Clothing journey full circle, and encapsulates my thinking and doing during the past five years. I do not know where it will lead, but I do know I will bring the learning along with me.

As you step out on a journey of your own, consider this quote:[66]

> Start where you are now and use what you already have to do what you can.

If it is a Slow Clothing journey, you might begin by appreciating the story behind the clothes you already own and taking some time to reflect before buying anew.

Learning from a Slow Clothing life

- **grow** – we are the sum of everything that went before

- **skills** – sewing and handmade skills are useful through life

- **accept** – embrace imperfection, life wasn't meant to be perfect

- **fibres** – natural fibres breathe, synthetic fibres are plastic

- **fabric** – linen is easy care if you don't iron, wool needs little washing

- **explore** – take time to follow rainbows, even if there is no pot of gold

- **consider** – buy with care, not on a whim or on special

- **reinvent** – all natural resources can have multiple uses

Until we make something for ourselves to wear, we cannot appreciate the resources, time and skill that go into the clothes we buy.

— Jane Milburn

Chapter 3

CREATIVITY

Discovering our own
Profiles from The Slow Clothing Project and Sew it Again

When we follow a pattern to the letter, we create something in another's shadow. When we explore our own creativity, something original emerges.

Creativity is within us all yet some use it more than others. Creativity is a free and renewable resource. We can tap into it through play, curiosity and experimentation. Creative problem solving and ingenuity are important life skills, as our future evolves with more complexity and less certainty.

Creative learning is best achieved in the course of working on projects as we learn to improvise, to adapt and hone our ability to understand and design solutions. Playful experimentation, trying new things, tinkering with materials and taking risks teaches us how to learn from our failures.[67]

There are endless ways to apply creativity in our lives. Individualism is arising and can't be outsourced! By developing a maker culture, we inject creativity and resourcefulness into our food, clothes, and homes.

Everyone is born creative, said textile artist Julie Paterson in her Imperfect Manifesto:

> Every day is an opportunity to perform a new creative act. Making things makes us feel good. We learn to do something by doing it. When we are brave our life expands. Risk is what transforms us. Imperfection is our ally.[68]

In her doctoral thesis, Dr Nicola Smith found DIY was part of an active search for meaning and experience through direct engagement with the physical world. She said creative freedom has been suppressed in an era when places, commodities and tools are almost entirely designed for us. Those who engage in DIY often do so to achieve self-actualisation and personal transformation.[69]

What better way to explore creativity than through the clothes we wear, that express our personality and character. Our garments become uniquely our own when we have a hand in their making. In the previous chapter, I touched on two projects to come from my social enterprise Textile Beat: Sew it Again and The

Jane wearing her upcycled t-shirt dress made for The Slow Clothing Project in 2016, at the South Mossman River in far north Queensland. Photo by Darcy Milburn.

Slow Clothing Project. In this chapter, I'd like to fire up your creativity by presenting thoughts from some of the makers I had the pleasure of coming across.

For all the blogs and inspiration revealed during my year-long daily Sew it Again challenge, go to www.sewitagain.com. All 40 stories from The Slow Clothing Project, demonstrating resourcefulness and creativity, are available on the Textile Beat website http://textilebeat.com/slow-clothing/.

The Slow Clothing Project

While this came after Sew It Again, I would first like to introduce you to some resourceful, thoughtful individuals I met during The Slow Clothing Project

who choose to create clothing to suit themselves for a range of reasons—to reflect their personal style, to wear something they feel comfortable in and connected to, or with a bigger goal such as reducing clothing waste.

We live in an era when clothing, accessories and other merchandise is almost entirely designed and made for us in a way that leaves little space to express our own creativity. While some people may want to dress to fit in and conform to accepted mores and fashion of the day, others prefer an individualistic approach and do not mind standing apart.

May their stories inspire you…

Level of everyday creativity	Motivations	Requirements (creativity + skill)	Design spaces	Everyday activities
Arranging	To select and possess	Minimal or no interest in creativity Minimal or no domain experience	Design for consuming	Shopping, buying, owning and using
Doing	To get something done/to be productive	Minimal interest Minimal domain experience	Design for experiencing	Doing and using
Adapting	To make something on my own	Some interest Some domain expertise	Design for adapting	Adapting, modifying, or filling in
Making	To make something with my own hands	Genuine interest Domain experience	Co-creating / Co-design	Making
Creating	To express my creativity	Passion Domain expertise	Co-creating / Co-design	Creating

This table from research by Dr Nicola Smith, see over, shows varying levels of engagement with creativity and design.

Dr Nicola Smith – lifestyles of simplicity

Based on years of research and hands-on engagement in creativity and DIY, Dr Nicola Smith believes there is enormous personal and environmental value in becoming a bricoleur (someone who uses whatever tools/ materials are at hand, with whatever skills they have or can learn; someone who becomes immersed in the moment, the practice, the *doing*).

'As a doctoral thesis topic, I researched how both professionals and DIYers set about improving their homes in the hope of living a better life, having the 'perfect' lifestyle. During the research it became clear that most people are locked in a daily struggle between wants and needs, resources and desires, creativity and consumption, and between real and imagined lives.

'The most valued DIY experiences were reported by those who had lifestyles of simplicity and practicality, of collaboration with others (family, friends), of constant creative challenges. The least satisfied were those driven by continual consumption, motivated by the resale market, the fear of being left behind.'

Nicola's research findings also suggested that in taking personal control over their immediate environment and shaping the way they live, people felt confident, competent and capable. DIY may provide an opportunity for self-growth and the capacity for embracing change.

'Novelty and the need to possess at the expense of creativity (doing), longevity and comfort has a lot to do with why so much clothing and home furnishing gets discarded—it is appealing on the hanger/in the display, but ultimately does not feel quite right next time it is worn, not comfortable, not appropriate, not in character.'

As she reflects on the influences that shaped her career and lifestyle, Nicola can now see that design, creativity, craft, DIY and 'hands on' landscape have been there since childhood.

The Slow Clothing Project provided a reason for Nicola to revisit her fabric stash and more op shops, and create a series of tops in keeping with her relaxed country style. 'What I created is now my absolutely most favourite top—simple, practical, comfortable, soft (no doubt from years in the wash and blowing on a line), lightweight and worn all the time with shorts/jeans/capri pants.'

Nicola's advice: 'Do not be too critical of your skills and imagination; it leads to procrastination. If you buy pre-loved clothing or sheets to experiment with, you are supporting a charity, keeping resources in a cycle of use for longer and not fuelling consumption. You are also keeping your own costs to a minimum which will help you feel less fearful of 'ruining' something and 'wasting' your money—a win/win.'

Julie Hillier – sharing handmade skills

Applying creativity within a framework is what Julie Hillier demonstrated through her Simply Sewn project using a simple pattern and resources to hand to create 10 different variations of one pattern.

Julie learned to sew by osmosis from her dressmaker mum. After experimenting with various patterns over the years and learning by making mistakes (and embracing them), she has settled on a few favourites and now uses them over and over. There is endless variety available simply by changing the type of fabric, the colour, the shape of a sleeve, the line of a skirt, and so on.

'I think we are hard-wired to be creative and that our emotional and spiritual well-being is enhanced when we use our hands to make. I still get a real thrill out of making my own garments. It's a combination of the fun of the actual sewing and then the joy of wearing something that you have made for yourself, something that fits well, suits your colouring and reflects your style and personality.'

Julie believes everyone should be able to sew on a button and re-hem their dress or pants. The 'slowness' of the handmade process allows people to focus on one task, move at a slower pace, engage their hands in a productive process all combined with creating something new.

Julie is concerned about the way in which garments now seem almost 'disposable' because they are getting cheaper and cheaper to buy. Fast fashion makes her sad. SAD for the makers who work in horrible conditions for a pittance, SAD for the huge waste that is being generated as people discard garment after garment that they probably have hardly worn because the clothing has less value to them because it was only cheap, SAD that we are establishing a culture that devalues the effort required to make something by hand, SAD that we are so consumption focused, ever-searching for that momentary high that comes with a new purchase and SAD that people have lost their role in the creative process of generating their own wardrobe.

She now works to empower others to use their hands through Brisbane-based Ministry of Handmade, which has Simply Sewn as one of its many creative workshops.

Julie's advice: Just start! Learn some basic skills, practise, be prepared to mess up a bit, keep going, enjoy the process, find some like-minded people, set aside dedicated time to progress your projects. Set realistic expectations, start with small simple projects and work from there to build confidence.

Julie shows nine of the 10 garments she made using the same simple pattern, showing how one pattern and various remnant pieces of fabric can be redeployed for a new life.

Elizabeth Kingston – wearing timeless styling

Dressing in a way that is never in, nor out, of fashion has great appeal to Elizabeth Kingston because she believes style endures while fashion is transient.

Elizabeth shares timeless styling ideas through her Instagram account @timeless_styling to help people shift their thinking from being 'in fashion' to being 'in style'.

That means there's no need for a new wardrobe every season, you just combine a range of pieces in your own way, applying your own style and imaginative thought.

'Creating unique pieces has always appealed to me. In more recent years, knowing that doing so is more eco-friendly and far more sustainable for our planet has fuelled this passion even more.

'I love embellishing the surface of my fabrics, and have found beading and/or the use of embroidery threads to be an excellent method of doing this.

'She believes makers need to publicly show and share their skills and examples of the art of sewing to demonstrate the usefulness of being able to create their own.

'Those who can't sew or choose not to learn can support artists and designers of handmade or specialist creations through purchase, as the next best option.

'I have always considered myself to be a maker—opting to make my own clothes, soft furnishings and at times accessories. Over the years I have dabbled in weaving, dyeing, printmaking, felt making and tassel making, bringing each of these into the creation of my garments and/or décor.'

Elizabeth's advice: Start simple. A basic commercial pattern is a great starting point, so that the general concept of the body and how pieces fit together in construction can be understood. An alternative to that is buying a second-hand garment or using an old favourite (which has seen better days), and unpicking it to then reconstruct it through modifications or use as a pattern to create a fresh new piece. Revisiting the same garment style using different fabrics and exploring alternatives is a fabulous way of gaining confidence in the development of your sewing skills and creativity. From there you can step up the degree of difficulty.

Elizabeth wears upcycled denim pinny (made at a Textile Beat workshop), while other garments show an embroidered white skirt that became a dress by adding embellished panels to hemline and shoulder straps, and a tablecloth transformed into a kaftan with tassels.

Kylie Challenor – sew like a professional editor

Kylie Challenor believes the magic of sewing is imagining what you want to create and a few hours later, there it is!

Self-taught as an adult, Kylie says she reaps many rewards—freedom of choice, flexibility of style, enjoyment and self-worth. She sews in a corner of the dining room of her two-bedroom unit—'we don't have a lot of space!'—and now her only purchases are the occasional pair of jeans, a band t-shirt or exercise gear.

Kylie had been reflecting for some time about fast fashion and consumer culture before she started her sewing journey. She'd read about sweatshops, was increasingly uncomfortable with the conditions in which people were working and wanted to drastically reduce her part in that.

'About six years ago I'd repurposed a dress from eBay for my wedding dress by having it altered by a local dressmaker. I decided that I wanted to have those skills too! A helpful and patient friend from the United States was visiting Australia at the time and helped guide me through making my first simple gathered skirt. From there, I deciphered patterns myself, asked Google, made mistakes and learned a lot about patience.

'When I started this journey, I wanted to end up having the ability to change a pattern to suit my tastes (rather than just following the instructions). It's taken a long time, but now I'm there! I recently made an absolutely gorgeous Japanese pattern in grey and black. I didn't like the puffy sleeves in the pattern, so I made a sleeveless version instead. Just like that, I can imagine what I want—and a few hours later, there it is!

'At the very least, having handmade skills contributes to my sense of self-worth. I feel proud when I make something I love, and I've been stopped in the street many times and asked where I got my dress. I also love the fact that I'm not impacting on anyone else's life negatively by having them work in dangerous conditions to make me nice things to wear.'

Kylie's advice: 'My first piece of advice is just give it a go. Yes, you will need patience. Yes, you will need to invest a little bit of time. Yes, you will make mistakes. But it will be worth it. I had no sewing skills whatsoever when I started. My second piece of advice is to stop asking your friends with sewing skills to make things for you (or to hem your pants). Unless you know they enjoy making things for other people (and/or you are willing to pay them for their time), stop being cheeky and learn to do it yourself. Or pay an alterationist, like I had to before I could sew!'

Leeyong Soo – making satisfaction

Leeyong Soo knows the palpable satisfaction of making and remaking her own clothes because she has been doing so for years. Although confessing to consumerist tendencies, Leeyong loves op shops and trawling through markets because she is attracted to things that are not mass-produced.

'Having shopped secondhand for many years now, I can't believe how easily people hand over huge amounts of money for clothing that was likely made in sweatshops and that they will possibly only wear a few times before it's out of fashion.

'I find Slow Clothing—pieces made from scratch or somehow customised—so much more interesting than high street fashion bought off the rack. I love rummaging at markets and opshops and finding things that no one else has and wondering about who wore them. I suppose it is also about the thrill of the chase—there are hundreds of the same piece on the racks at chain stores but at an op shop, whatever you find is generally one-of-a-kind and not necessarily going to be in your size.'

Leeyong believes that when people spend time making things by hand, they tend to value them more than if they just bought them: 'Making something by hand gives people a sense of satisfaction. There are plenty of studies that show crafting is akin to meditation and is great for building confidence and social connections.'

Leeyong learned to sew through trial and error and her philosophy is simple. As long as it looks OK from the outside and is sturdy enough to wear, she is not too fussed how well it is finished on the inside. A girl after my own heart!

The garment Leeyong created for The Slow Clothing Project shows how truly clever and resourceful she is. 'I was gifted a long hooded kaftan made from printed cotton and used the lower part of it to make a simple shift dress but still had the top section left over. I used the bodice section as the garment base then created detachable ruffles and peplum from the sleeves and hood section, so the garment can be worn several ways. So from one big kaftan, I have made five garments!'

Leeyong mends things—clothes and objects alike—rather than throwing them out and keeps objects that can be used to make other things. Read more on her blog stylewilderness.com

Leeyong's advice: 'When you're starting out, try little alterations such as adding trims, patches and pockets to things, and then you can work up to making things completely from scratch. Once you start sewing your own clothes you'll get to know your body shape better and develop your sense of style.'

Photo by
Jo Hammond

Paisley Park – a conscious maker

Paisley Park was raised to be conscious of all that surrounds her, including food, clothing, impacts on people and the environment. As a child her clothes were either made by her mother, hand-me-downs or from charity shops. She was never interested in fashion and the idea of creating comfortable practical clothing that can be worn for years greatly appealed.

'I taught myself to sew when I came out of hospital in 2011. Since then I have become a full-time seamstress and sewing teacher alongside my label (Pixie in the Park). It has been shown that people with hobbies, pets, faith and so-on have better mental health, which in turn impacts society positively; I also believe that engaging people in a creative skill can increase their desire to learn further about how items are created.

'The most common phrases I hear from my students are "I can't believe how long it takes to make a dress" and "this is harder than I thought it would be". I am often able to then open up communication about the fast fashion industry and get people to look at the labels in their clothing and discuss the manufacturing conditions of their clothing. People are most often fascinated, disgusted and empathetic. This then helps people become more resilient through learning ways to adapt, to live within their means, and reduce consumption, spending and debt.'

For The Slow Clothing Project, Paisley turned remnants from her organic cotton t-shirt line into patchwork fabric in the general shape of the pattern pieces she was using and then made the dress. 'I added hemp panels to shoulders to prevent warping with the weight of the dress, and finished it with handmade cotton bias. I liked the dress the 'right way' and others liked it 'inside out' so it has now become a reversible dress.'

'Where I live, in far north Queensland, you cannot have more than a handful of garments due to the environment, so I have learnt to have two weeks' worth of clothing and no more. This means my clothing must be resilient, comfortable and very practical.

'For me, the idea that I can wear the same item of clothing repeatedly for years is exciting. I feel that my clothing is designed to not only be useful but also that each piece is a work of art and I enjoy being able to share my art daily.'

Paisley's advice: 'Jump in, see what you can create, learn about your machine and your fabrics and I highly recommend finding a one-on-one teacher or mentor whom you enjoy working with, to explain a few things that are harder to learn alone. Having someone to interact with, learn from and question can speed up your skill development exponentially and enable you to be more creative, quicker, which is even more rewarding.'

Cath Jarvis – valuing sewing skills

Cath Jarvis is a busy sonographer and mother of three who, with partner Kevin, runs a sheep property 'Kia-Ora' at Tottenham in central New South Wales.

Growing up, Cath's mum encouraged her three daughters to sidestep domestic tasks and focus instead on professional and less-traditional work. The girls rode motorbikes and horses, and generally mucked around on the farm. It wasn't until she heard about the Sew it Again project that Cath realised that being able to sew could be very handy. 'I googled Jane and well, as they say, the rest is history.'

'I love tinkering with old fabric and trying to make something new out of it. I love collecting old tea towels and doilies and just playing to see what they might lend themselves to. I have changed my whole mindset now about not just mending clothing but also reusing them to make another garment.

'I've also enjoyed experimenting with making natural plant dyes. The ironbark trees on the farm make a really rich red dye when you soak the bark. Kevin can remember his mother and grandmother making dye from bark and leaves—it is a pity to lose these skills between generations.

'I think we need to be more conscious of how much of the world's resources go into making all these clothes that we don't really need. And of course, I would love to see us using more natural fibres like cotton and wool instead of fabrics made from plastic.'

For The Slow Clothing Project, Cath made a denim pinafore from three of her children's outgrown jeans, a well-worn denim skirt of her own that was beyond repair, and a pair of Kevin's torn work shorts. She used the pinny pattern in Chapter 5 and preserved interesting details like labels and metal buttons.

The pinny is a wearable statement about sustainable living. 'When you live in a remote location like we do, we tend to 'make do' with what we have. Farmers have been repairing and inventing since the beginning of time.

'We all have too much stuff, we have reached the tipping point now where so much of what we do is no longer sustainable, and we need to make a few changes to our lifestyles. If we could all just mend our clothes instead of throwing them out and buying new, the planet would say thank you. Sewing is a very mindful activity. You can forget about all the other stuff going on in the background and just sew.'

Cath's advice: 'Just have a go, what's the worst thing that could happen? Try to find some like-minded people to bounce your ideas off because it is fun to sew in a group.'

Libby Woodhams – artful clothing

Dr Libby Woodhams began making clothes because she couldn't buy anything she found sufficiently colourful and different. She doesn't consider herself a dressmaker because she mostly sews straight lines and lacks patience for tailoring. Libby buys patterns with simple shapes and finds Kwik Sew patterns suit her skills and provide a good canvas for appliqué or fabric painting. Some of Libby's staple 'makes' are a patchwork skirt with elastic waistband and patchwork coats.

'I like making coats to cover a multitude of sins and the clothes underneath can be very simple and timeless. I try to wear as much merino as possible because I think wool is the best fabric for sub-tropical climates.

'Coming from a family of woolgrowers, I'm naturally an advocate for wearing merino. It is a wonderful fabric that avoids many of the pitfalls of cotton, silk and linen—it absorbs moisture without getting wet, it resists creasing and crushing so no ironing is required, and it repels odours which means that garments can be worn for longer without needing laundering. And, most modern merino garments can be washed in cold water in a washing machine.'

For The Slow Clothing Project, Libby created a reversible wrap skirt which enables different looks and is flattering for diverse body shapes. On one side, she used fabric pieces reclaimed from men's merino trousers from an op shop. The reverse side is a patchwork of hand-painted and block-printed fabrics, scraps from other projects and remnants. To fasten it, she used an old tie given to her by a retired friend and sewed buttonholes at the different size markers, adding two buttons to accommodate a range of sizes. It's a skirt with a story!

With a background in creative expression, Libby is an advocate for the healing benefits of making things with our hands: when hands are occupied, enriching conversations somehow happen almost involuntarily.

Reflecting on changes in recent decades, Libby says: 'I really dislike that globalisation means it doesn't matter where I am in the world, all the shops are the same and all the clothes are the same. In my view, it makes it even more important to seek out and support the local designers who are making something different.'

Libby's advice: 'Buy the best sewing machine you can afford because they sew better, last longer, and are easier to use and maintain. Buy from a shop where the staff sew and can help with advice, and do the workshop and/or lessons that should come with the purchase of a machine. Use natural woven fabrics to start with because they are easier to sew than jerseys and synthetics which can slip and slide all over the place. And, finally, don't be afraid to ask for help even if it seems like a kindergarten problem.'

Eliza Kelly – dressing with a difference

Slow Clothing is a different way of dressing and thinking about clothing, says teenager Eliza Kelly.

'The attitude of the world these days seems to be that 'new is better', and 'more, more, more', but I think that there is so much beauty, uniqueness and stories in recycled and re-modelled clothing. There is so much to be gained by recycling and re-using the materials that we have been given, and changing things with older fit, style or fashion to be useable today and tomorrow.'

'It is exciting to think that I can dress in a way that uses old, or out-of-fashion clothing to make something new. I love the way that I can create something original, unique and different. Isn't it awesome when someone says 'what a nice ...... where did you get it?' and I can say that I made it! It makes me warm on the inside when I know that I have recycled something and given it another life.'

Eliza believes there is huge value in using your hands to create. 'It is not only the end product that is so worthwhile (which I totally agree holds its own value) but the process of using your imagination, creativity, skills, some thread and a needle, to turn a few scraps of fabric into something useful—turning not a lot into a new useful item! The actual act of creating a product also gives the maker satisfaction and self-worth—something that is being searched for in today's society.

'Using your hands (whether it be woodwork, sewing, welding—whatever!) and taking the time to slow down, and put time and effort into making and producing something unique is rare in this day and age of consumerism where most things are cheap and bulk manufactured.'

Homeschooled and shown to sew by her mum, grandmothers (and the Internet), Eliza places great stock in testing her creativity, imagination, innovation and individuality.

Eliza's Slow Clothing project was an A-line, 13-panel denim wrap-around skirt from pieces of old jeans. She teamed this with a denim shirt that she had trimmed to suit herself.

Eliza's advice: 'Just have a go! It's amazing what you can do with just a needle and thread or sewing machine! Let's be honest, often when I make my own clothing, it isn't perfect or flawless, it's handmade—and you can usually tell! The handmade look makes them original. This can be off-putting for those who want their clothes to look 'just right', perhaps 'normal'. But I remind myself that home-made clothes are not shop-bought, and we don't pretend they are. Making your own clothes is a journey, not a destination.'

Kate Fletcher – eclectic and sustainable style

Kate Fletcher has been making and recycling clothing as long as she can remember. And for the past decade, she has organised a sustainable clothing show in Tasmania as a response to growing awareness of the environmental and social impacts of the global clothing industry.

Kate's individual style is influenced by people at home and abroad, many of whom she has met through the international volunteer program Willing Workers On Organic Farms (WWOOF).

'I am always darning, patching and dyeing fabrics and garments. I often have a number of wwoofers staying and we create garments together. My motivation is doing whatever it takes to keep garments looking great, in circulation and away from landfill. I also enjoy networking and sharing ideas, skills and resources. We grow things to eat and forage for the dyepot and table. We network and share. I model what I think is important and what works for the planet.

'I have a very eclectic wardrobe, mainly handmade, upcycled, recycled and second-hand clothing. I trade in these things so I have access to a wide variety of raw materials. My most typical raw materials are blankets, sheets, curtains, tablecloths and doilies. I prefer natural fabrics. My favourite unusual find recently was a cloth meat bag which covered a whole lamb carcass.

'I make stuff all the time and most often the way I acquire new clothing is when I make or dye something for our Salamanca Market stall and it fits me, so I keep it, or a wwoofer makes or dyes something I like. I enjoy thinking about the people who made the garments when I wear them.'

The story Kate tells about her Slow Clothing Project epitomises the difference between slow clothing and fast fashion. 'I gathered beautiful scraps from previous dyeing projects which carry memories of friends from across the world and stitched them together in various places and with various people. I have ended up with a rich tapestry and a beautiful journey which money could not buy. It started life as a cream blanket and is stitched with op shop-found thread which I dyed.'

Kate believes fast fashion and the culture of consumerism is sad and soulless. 'I want people to think about this and give up believing that buying a new garment so cheaply that they can just throw it out without a care—is not smart or sustainable. One thing I am concerned about is textile workers having a living wage.'

Kate's advice: 'Create together. The magic of a creative life is sharing it with people you love, then you get to love them even more because of what you share together.'

Vivienne Poon – coining a garment

Knowing the story behind the garment is a certainty when you've made it yourself. When you've been creative and resourceful in the making then you are wearing something totally unique.

Such was the case when a friend gave Vivienne Poon some 1936 Fiji pennies and she set about developing a design to incorporate them in a bodice featuring two-coin tassels which chink when she walks, and a hemline with one-coin tassels that are not too weighty.

Vivienne enjoyed making new from old, the challenge of using remnants and found bits of materials, and the opportunity to create and recreate in limitless ways. 'Textiles was compulsory in my undergraduate Art course and I enjoyed learning about tailoring and technical aspects, embroidery and creating items. As a teacher, I always insisted on teaching in both Textiles and Art as they are complementary.

'Both my grandmothers sewed, and I still have the family treadle machine. My mother, who lived through WW II on ration cards, taught me to unpick hand-knitted garments to reknit, and salvage dress fabrics which were made into polishing cloths and floor cloths.

'After sewing for two sons, which was fun but limited, I had years of sewing for my twin daughters. This was so exciting, creating 'same but different' clothing in mix and match colours, from casual to 'good' clothes, plus creating a huge wardrobe of dress-up clothing for them from pre-school age to adulthood.'

Vivienne became involved in The Slow Clothing Project as a way to influence positive change. She believes that 'making' will be the new 'doing'. 'I want to spark or reignite interest amongst family and friends to re-create beauty and personal items especially from old fabrics and to encourage others to be creators. My latest trend is to create an entire outfit after purchasing one element, and use this piece as a starting point for my own story. This provides me with a springboard for ideas, and allows me scope to divert and create.'

'The process to make this garment was slow! Research was required to work out how to incorporate the coins from a designer's viewpoint and the method of attaching the coins. In my research, I found that coins needed to dangle from their own string; an insertion into a seam was the obvious place. But I didn't want coins dangling at a hem edge or looking like a Bollywood outfit. I adapted a contemporary pattern, instead of purchasing a new pattern, which is all part of the slow clothing ideal.'

Vivienne's advice: 'Practise whatever has been learned. Do not just make one item, make more and repeat the learning so that the learning becomes second nature.'

Mariana Kirova – an agent for change

Mariana Kirova is a professional upcycler who transforms rescued clothing into unique timeless pieces through Eco Fashion Sewing, a business she established after studying fashion design in Western Australia.

'When I was exposed to fast fashion during my studies, I was stunned, disgusted and felt pain envisioning poor exhausted workers and greedy-for-profits managers and shareholders. I think of my son and his future children and their children. The apocalyptic vision of what we are going to leave them squeezes my chest and my heart stops. I don't want that future for him.'

Mariana's passion for sewing was triggered from the love for fabric scraps as a child growing up in the small, now post-communist European country, Bulgaria. 'A beautiful little piece of heaven nature-wise, but we didn't have abundance of pretty and shiny things in the shops. At that time, I now know, I fell in love with creating.'

'Coming to live in Australia with my husband and son about seven years ago, I got back into sewing again. I bought a second-hand domestic sewing machine and began learning from the Internet. I studied fashion and my clothes-making journey began.

'I believe the most accessible way for me to be eco-friendly is to buy second hand, because of the time involved in making. I admire The Slow Clothing Project because it gathers sewing lovers who are rejecting irresponsible mass production and overconsumption. We need more projects that endorse handmade and DIY, natural and eco-conscious.

'For my garment, I wanted to demonstrate that even boring clothing articles like men's button-up shirts could be transformed into interesting and unique women's fashion. We can pursue 'to become' instead of 'to have and acquire' which the process of creating by being eco-caring is doing. Slow for me means eco-friendly, natural and buy less. So, whenever it's possible, my family and I are applying that philosophy.

'People don't need to have the latest car, sophisticated gadgets or a luxurious house. It is the system assumption, but not necessarily our real life situation and way of thinking.'

Mariana's advice: 'Ignore trends, it narrows imagination. Although time-consuming and sometimes challenging, making your own clothes is invaluable. It gives pleasure and a sense of achievement, which boosts your self-confidence and self-belief, and makes a good swap for psychotherapy. Remember that no shopping therapy can give you even a tiny bit of this feeling!'

Emma Williamson – handmade purpose

Emma Williamson believes handmade skills can contribute to sustainability and resilience because they help people feel they have something worthwhile to contribute to the world. It affords them confidence, pride and enables them to make a living while also supporting a richness of cultures.

Formally trained to sew at the Sydney Institute of TAFE, Ultimo, Emma says: 'The Slow Clothing movement interests me for its potential to reduce our unsustainable consumption patterns. It really has a positive impact on the environment when we reuse instead of buying new. I think the engagement people are having with slow clothing practices is not only empowering at an individual level, it's eye-opening for change at a community level.

'From my experience in the fashion industry in metropolitan and international arenas, I have become conscious of unethical methods in terms of human input, which are all too often involved in the production of fast fashion.

'I see slow fashion creating an alternative outside of, and in opposition to, this mode of placing continuous skyrocketing pressure on human and natural resources. To me this is beyond worthwhile: it's imperative.'

A collector of pre-loved tablecloths, tea towels, doilies and wall-hangings, picked up at op shops, along with "failed" projects rescued from fellow creatives, Emma believes in applying the "slow" philosophy to almost every facet of life. 'At its core, it is advocating slowing down life's pace.'

Emma created her Slow Clothing Project garment from a surplus cotton sheet, left behind by a former tenant in her rented apartment, and a length of elastic: 'I wanted to save this sheet, to recycle it into something beautiful so it could continue its life in a useful way. The big and bold character of the garment came about organically, a product of simply having so much fabric to work with. I only sewed two seams to get this finished piece.'

Emma's advice: 'Don't try to think and plan too much. Start with something simple and you'll be amazed how much the process and your mistakes help you out. It's likely you'll depart from your original idea and end up with something you never imagined you could come up with!'

Inspired? It is great to wear a good story, doubly so when you created it yourself. The overwhelming message, repeated often in these maker stories, is to just give it a go. Learning comes from doing.

Sew it Again 2014

My Sew it Again project was a year of learning by doing. At the time I wrote:

> 'I've been rescuing discarded natural-fibre clothing from op shops and other sources for years because I value them as natural resources … I plan to make a daily ritual of upcycling garments from my own and others' wardrobes as a way of creating and sharing a different way of dressing that is mindful of the Earth's finite resources.'

I aimed to demonstrate we can be empowered, sustainable and thrifty when we use clothing already in circulation rather than buying new. The project became a public commitment when I was interviewed by Brisbane broadcaster Rebecca Levingston in December 2013 and Tim Cox conducted a follow-up interview in January 2015.[70]

Below is a selection of the revelations, insights and ideas I found while blogging every day.

Sew 6: New York photographer Bill Cunningham[71] described fashion as the armour to survive everyday life, and dressing the body as an artform. His own armour included a plastic poncho (tears held together with black gaffer tape) and utilitarian blue shirts.

Sew 8: We do not need to make complex clothing from scratch when there's a high likelihood of failure but it is handy to know how to sew on a button, mend or alter a hem, and make basic

Rebecca Levingston with Jane Milburn in the ABC Brisbane studios.

adaptions to extend the life of our clothing. Being able to sew is empowering—it gives us choices in the garments we wear because we are not restricted to what we can buy in stores or online. When we sew, we can change styles and shapes to flatter. Refashioning requires a little time and ingenuity, but expands choices and develops creativity.

Sew 18: For everyone, clothing is essential. As well-known Australian designer and champion of natural fibres Liz Davenport has been known to say, you can get to an event without a car and without breakfast—but not without clothes.

Sew 19: Creativity is an interesting quality. The *Macquarie Dictionary* defines it as the state or quality of being creative. Creative, adj, 1. having the quality or power of creating. 2. resulting from originality of thought or expression. 3. originative; productive.

Thought leader Deepak Chopra identified creativity as one of the most significant spiritual laws in *The seven spiritual laws of superheroes*.

Chopra defines creativity as a leap in consciousness that brings new meaning or new context to any situation or problem. Cultivating creativity turns problems and obstacles into challenges and opportunities. In every adversity there is a seed of something magnificent. He says creativity is the principal force that drives all life, evolution and the mechanics of science. To effectively harness creativity and lead in your life, Chopra recommends:

1. Determine what to get rid of—what in your life detracts from its quality? Commit to letting go of whatever it is that is holding you back, including toxic habits, emotions, relationships, substances and environments.

2. Practice clarity of vision—what do you want to create? Ask yourself what you really want, why you really want it, and if manifesting it will serve a higher purpose for humanity

3. Follow nine steps to accessing creativity with diligence and detachment. These are: intended outcome; information gathering; information analysis; incubation; insight; inspiration; implementation; integration and incarnation.

Sew 47: Another day, another great read—this time *Eco chic: The savvy shoppers guide to ethical fashion* by Matilda Lee, editor of the Green Pages of the Ecologist magazine. In her chapter on DIY fashion, Lee writes: 'For a variety of reasons, the self-sufficiency once so valued in generations past now seems outdated and unnecessary. This is a shame because mending, sewing and refashioning are weapons in an arsenal of skills on how to revitatlise and individualise a dulling wardrobe. Even those among us with the most bulging clothes racks at some point wake up and find that they have 'nothing to wear'. Instead of rushing out to buy something new, giving old clothes—whether your own or someone else's—a second lease of life can be more satisfying and add to a more distinct wardrobe.'

Sew 49: Lee quotes Mrs Hubert Humphrey, wife of former US vice-president: 'When a woman learns to sew, she becomes more fashion-conscious than if she just goes out and buys what she wants.'

Sew 52: Nothing is ever entirely original in this world: it just evolves from something or somewhere. In his book *Think! Before it's too late*, Edward De Bono says the human brain is designed to set up routine patterns and to use and follow these patterns. He says all valuable creative ideas will be logical in hindsight. Creativity is not a mysterious gift or special talent—it is the behaviour of a self-organising information system that makes asymmetric patterns (the brain).

'It need no longer be a matter of sitting and waiting for ideas and inspiration. We can do certain things that will result in the brain having new ideas. This is a big step forwards in the history of mankind,' says de Bono.

Sew 70: We know charity op shops are filled with perfectly good clothing. After pondering why so many quality garments are being moved on, I've come up with a theory. People are literally outgrowing them and need to upsize. Bingo. There's an obvious correlation between our bulging waistlines and the burgeoning mountain of waste clothing. Australia is ranked as one of the fattest nations in the developed world, with three in five people (over 60 per cent) now overweight.

Sew 72: On the first anniversary of the Rana Plaza factory collapse, April 24, 2014, readers were encouraged to think about the growing global Fashion Revolution:

• We want you to wear an item of clothing inside out because we want people to change the way they look at the clothes they wear. **Be curious.**

- We want you to start asking 'who made my clothes?' in order to initiate human connections throughout the supply chain. **Find out**.

- We want hundreds of thousands of people to make that gesture which will, in turn, raise awareness within the fashion industry that they need to continue the process of change. **Do something about it.**

Sew 97: No problem can be solved from the same level of consciousness that created it: Albert Einstein.[72]

Sew 98: Fast fashion fosters a wear and toss approach to modern dress in the never-ending search for satisfaction from material consumption. More meaningful and realistic approaches to fashion have been studied and distilled into beautiful words by the Local Wisdom project out of the United Kingdom's Centre for Sustainable Fashion.[73] By exploring our relationship with clothes, researchers unearthed themes of usership based on people's stories. You can view these words in pictures via *The Guardian*[74], the source of the following words:

Patina of use: with our garments, as with our bodies, the passing of time leaves its mark. With clothes, we sometimes discard pieces because they are ageing, dated, jaded or worn; at other times we buy vintage pieces, coveting that which looks old. Yet these both overlook the power and pleasure of marking the passing of time as it is recorded in our clothes; the forging of memories, building of knowledge, evolution of appearance.

Alternative dress codes: the choices we make about what we wear are influenced by life present, lives past and our ideas about our future selves. Expressions of values, aspirations, heritage, understanding and the physical shape of our bodies build a rationale for dress that transcend narrow commercial views about fashion.

Transfer of ownership: giving a garment to someone else is sometimes a straightforward and spontaneous act and at other times more circuitous. The overlapping of ownership can embed a garment with memories.

Skills of resourcefulness: Creative activists contribute greatly to society through innovation and experimention. Their work is a training ground for new practices, for trialling novel approaches and reviving old skills that promote alternative ideas about fashion provision and consumption.

Sew 99: Green thrift describes the action of upcycling old stuff for ecological and financial health… and wellbeing. Refashioning clothing that already exists makes good sense. The hard work has been done (zips, buttons, hems already in place), resources expended (cotton grown and spun, fabric woven and dyed) and dollars already spent when items were newly purchased.

We think new clothes will boost our spirits and maybe they do for a while, but ultimately it is the body (and the mind) in them that determines wellbeing. When you open your mind to the creative possibilities that exist within your wardrobe (or your friends' or a nearby op shop)

Nurturing creativity

the sky is the limit if you apply a few simple skills and techniques for adapting them to suit *you*.

The gorgeous books by New York academic Sass Brown *Eco fashion* and *Refashioned* are full of creative inspiration from upcyclers around the world. Just by looking at the pictures, inspiration rubs off on the reader.

Sew 101: Upcycling natural fibre clothing for a second life makes sense—for the planet, the hip-pocket and personal satisfaction. There's recreation to be had in recreating new garments out of old. It is fun engaging one's creative and thrifty instincts, exploring and playing with textures and techniques—but it does require a willingness and flexibility to invest time in the process.

One of the most valuable things about having basic sewing skills is the independence and individuality they provide. You are not restricted to what's currently trendy and newly available online or in shops.

Sew 125: Uncertainty is an essential element of creativity, which in turn comes from mindful attention to your craft of choice. Harvard psychologist Dr Ellen Langer says our current culture leads us to try to minimise uncertainty, leading to mindless rigid behaviour governed by rules and routines. On the other hand, if we exploit the power of uncertainty we learn that things can become more than we previously thought possible. Mindfulness makes us sensitive to context, perspective, and changing situations.

Sew 129: The most common reason we hesitate when given a chance to express ourselves creatively is our fear of other people's negative opinions, according to Dr Langer. In her book *On becoming an artist*, Langer said while it was hard to try something without knowing the outcome, from a creative perspective, the unknown was actually preferable. Langer made the point that others' evaluations—good or bad—were not really objective and need not shape our choices: 'Evaluation is central to the way we make sense of our world; almost all of our thoughts are concerned with whether what we or others are doing or thinking is good or bad … If a change in our attitude about evaluation is to happen, the most important understanding we need to gain is that all behaviour makes sense from the actor's perspective or the actor wouldn't do it'.

Langer said most of us failed to engage in creative endeavours as meaningfully as we might, or even declined to involve ourselves in them altogether, because the risk of making mistakes was too great. But if we don't begin with a rigid plan, it is hard to make a mistake.

Sew 143*:* How about this for an amazing statistic—China's annual consumption of tissues is about 4.4 million tonnes. This has led to an Eco-Handkerchief event around the use of handkerchiefs over tissues as part of an eco-business trade mission to China from Australia to promote sustainable and environmentally friendly products to a 'green-hungry' Chinese market.

So many things that were once considered old-fashioned and traditional are returning to the forefront because we recognise them as 'eco-friendly', sustainable and practical ways of living.

Sew 147: Forecasting social-cultural trends is something European trendsetter Lidewij Edelkoort learned to do by trusting her instincts and she now travels the world presenting at events[75]. In Sydney, Australia, Edelkoort reflected on the current move towards nature, organics and the traditional. 'We're seeing the dawning of an embryonic age, where the social mood is shifting to a climate of community, care and compassion. A new epoch with different and more wholesome, localised options … Twenty years ago we craved imported goods. Now we're turning our attention to things that are local and locally made … We went very quickly into the desire for global things and I think we will also unglobalise rapidly which I think is positive because transportation is taking its toll on society, financially and ecologically. So if we can do less of that, the better it is.'

Sew 161: Self-reliance is a useful characteristic in life that springs from creativity, versatility, intuition, access to raw materials, knowledge and skills.

In the office, it means you can nut-out a pragmatic solution for a tricky problem. In the kitchen, it means you can pull together a feed without necessarily having all ingredients listed in a recipe. And in the clothing department, it means you can bring together disparate items and adapt them to suit yourself.

Sew 218: In the 21st century, society needs people who think creatively because as they step into

life's problems they are more able to find creative ways of dealing with them. That's a paraphrase of the *Life at 9* life journey television series[76] about creativity. It seems creativity is a predictor of success in every domain of life because it is problem-solving, divergent thinking of possible solutions when presented with a difficult issue.

As we grow up, we are often obliged to subvert our creativity, to conform and follow rules and the experts in this program suggested that our current education system's emphasis on performance and getting the 'right answer' is squashing creative development. Creativity is about taking risks, thinking out-of-the-box, being able to tolerate uncertainty—and it is enhanced through practise.

Sew 358: When we think of creativity, most think of art with a capital A, when really it is about having a sense of festivity, fun and playfulness. One of my academic friends says play is what she most enjoys about Sew it Again because we need more creative play in our lives and workplaces.

I was thrilled that Sew it Again was judged Social Media category winner in the Excellence in Rural Journalism 2015 Awards[77] by the Rural Press Club of Queensland. The judges' comments were:

> Jane Milburn's Sew It Again project engaged with the community, had a call to action and was transformative. It actually made a difference in the world.

Let's make that difference together, following what I have called the Slow Clothing Manifesto.

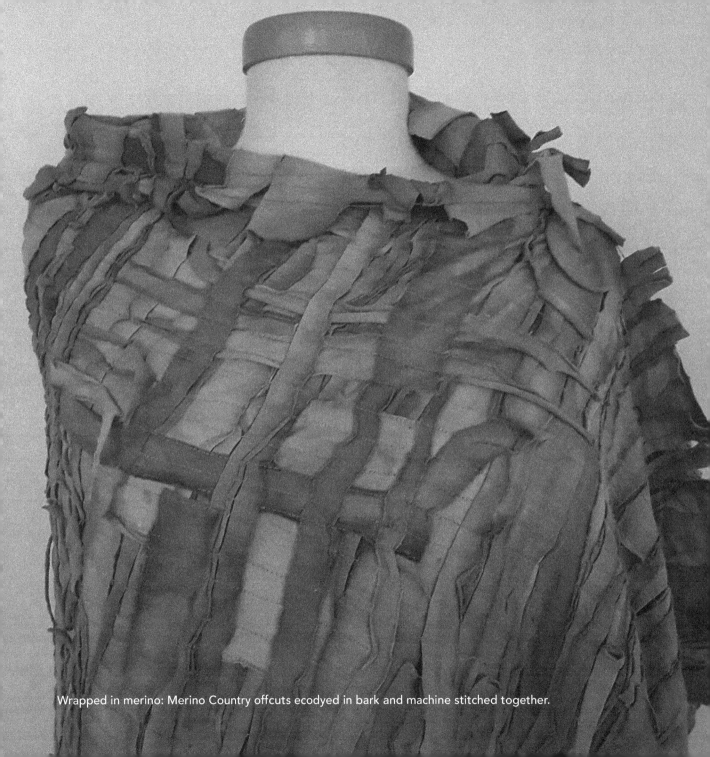

Wrapped in merino: Merino Country offcuts ecodyed in bark and machine stitched together.

Chapter 4

ACTIONS

The Slow Clothing Manifesto

Ways to thrive in a material world: think, natural, quality, local, few, care, make, revive, adapt, salvage

Slow Clothing is a way of thinking about and choosing clothes to ensure they bring meaning, value and joy to every day. It is about thoughtful, ethical, creative and sustainable ways of dressing while minimising our material footprint on the world.

With rising international concern about the state of planetary health[78], it is time to consider how we can adapt every day practices of eating, dressing and working to be more sustainable. While we particularly focus here on dressing, reflecting on consumption choices is relevant across all aspects of life because nothing should be bought without thought.

There are still only 365 days in the year, yet we may have up to four times the clothing we once did (as indicated by the data in Chapter 1). We might have an average of 150 items in our wardrobe, wear less than half of them regularly and spend about 15 minutes each day deciding what to wear, according to a UK study[79] (personally I find it helps to decide what to wear the next morning, before I go to bed). Most of us (62 per cent) have clothes in our wardrobe that have never been worn and about one-quarter of our wardrobe (23 per cent) is never or rarely worn, according to an Australian study.[80]

During our lifetime our style, shape and needs change. We go through stages of searching for newer, fresher looks and may use clothes to camouflage ourselves or attract attention. Or, we might choose one style or colour to become our uniform.

Hopefully as we move through life we shed the idea of perfection and learn to embrace clothes as friends that enable us to express our authentic self. This happens when we stop comparing ourselves with others and let go of the culture of envy which luxury fashion marketers play on, and prey on.

By developing self-awareness, we can create an independent style that reflects our uniqueness, our kansei. We can cherry-pick ideas from what we see around us, but need not be beholden to them.

SLOW CLOTHING manifesto

think	make thoughtful, ethical, informed choices
natural	treasure fibres from nature and limit synthetics
quality	buy well once, quality remains after price is forgotten
local	support local makers, those with good stories and fair trade
few	live with less, have a signature style, minimal wardrobe, unfollow
care	mend, patch, sort, sponge, wash less, use cold water, line dry
make	learn how to sew as a life skill, value DIY and handmade
revive	enjoy vintage, exchange, pre-loved, and swapping
adapt	upcycle, refashion, eco-dye, create new from old
salvage	donate, pass on, rag, weave, recycle or compost

Show up as
your natural,
authentic self.

– anything else is contrived.

— Jane Milburn

Slow Clothing values personal connection to garments through the stories and memories they hold. It considers the ethics and sustainability of our garments, their comfort and longevity, and our desire to be more engaged with the making process.

Slow Clothing strategies

The clothes we choose make a statement of who we are. They are a big part of our lives because we dress at least once every day. Clothes can cause us stress, clutter up our living space and soak up time.

There is no one way to go about restructuring your wardrobe collection. We arrive at our own solution, based on our age and stage. At all stages though, *less is indeed more.*

I love the approach of Japanese organiser extraordinaire Marie Kondo who recommends keeping only the clothes you totally love and treating them like friends by giving them space and order. (I confess here to being a hoarder: I keep all natural-fibre garments for future upcycling.)

Here's my suggested process for action:

1. Stop buying for a while

Random unplanned purchases are rarely useful. Pause for reflection. Watch *The True Cost*[81] documentary to understand why a culture change is needed for social, ethical and environmental reasons.

A period of not buying gives you space to think about what you already own, and how much you really need. I know quite a few people (including myself) who have gone a year or more without buying but you don't need to be that extreme.

Keeping a stable weight makes a big difference to the length of time clothes are useful in your wardrobe, so this is a time to reflect on where you are at on that front.

2. Study your style—shape, colour, image

We can all create our own individual style. There's even a wikihow[82] website to help! You don't have to follow what others do or promote—unless it suits you. Your style is influenced by the work you do and your stage of life. Developing your style is a personal journey. You can learn through experimentation, then stepping back from yourself as you look in the mirror. When you become confident in your own style, you are no longer a slave to fashion trends.

Shape: Accept and embrace who you are. This has never been more important, as the Body Image Movement attests.[83] We are all individuals and the vast majority of us are not model-thin or tall. We don't just vary in height and weight, we have different vertical shapes based on our leg and body length. Be assured there are ways to play up and play down various body parts, so check in with a stylist or image consultant if you aren't sure.

Colour: The colour tone of our skin has a huge influence on what clothing colours work best for us. We have either blue or yellow skin tones and are one of four seasons (blue tones are winter/summer, yellow tones are spring/autumn).[84] Within that we each have specific colours that throw light on our face that gives us a glow. When you know your best colours you don't always need to follow the recommendations but at least you can factor it in, particularly when making investment purchases.

Image: This will vary depending on the work you are doing at the time. There are two genres that reflect personality types—although obviously plenty of variation within.

> Contained look: This look is a more fitted, structured, neat, and uses colour judiciously. We see this mostly in formal workplaces.

> Expressive look: This look is more free-form, less fitted, random hems, more creative shapes and colour combos.

You will most likely know the image you want to project. It is possible you may have both these looks in your wardrobe. Go with your heart: which garments make you *feel* good.

If in doubt, choose to wear simple, functional clothing as a quiet statement of resistance to consumer culture. You can reinvent your image at any time.

3. Sort and curate existing wardrobe

Examine what you already have and consider what you want to shed, repair, refashion or put in storage. We need occasional audits—at least once or twice

a year—with the changing season of winter and summer. Once you get organised this might just involve a straighten-up, and a little weeding-out.

For the initial sort, create piles: keep, mend/adjust, donate, cut-up and bin. To help with decision-making, set aside time to try on and experiment with different combinations of tops and bottoms. Try on shoes and accessories too.

If you are interested in upcycling it is handy to find a space to store everything that has potential for repurposing. I've kept clothes from the thin-ish and not-so-thin times in my life which come in and out of favour.

Arrange the treasure you are keeping in a way that works for you. I have glass-fronted book shelves that house all my clothes that don't need to be on hangers. These garments are mostly knits, rolled up and arranged by category, and then by colour.

4. Seek out responsible choices

The challenge now is to make every future purchase a winner that will serve you well. You will feel better when you dress with conscience, in clothes that have a good story about how they came to be in your wardrobe. Buy on ethics, not on price. Aim to buy secondhand first: it is a great way to test what works best for you and to try new styles for little outlay. Choose clothes with flexible sizing, perhaps with elastic waists or adjustable straps, as this will extend their usefulness. Avoid fashion fads and passing trends—they are for followers not pioneers.

Slow Clothing Manifesto

Once you have your existing wardrobe honed, you can move forward with a more planned approach using the Slow Clothing Manifesto's 10 simple actions. I developed this framework as a process of thinking about how we can survive and thrive in a material world, and become more conscious of what we are wearing. It is not rocket science—these actions might once have been learned at school or passed on from one generation to the next.

The actions are: think, natural, quality, local, few, care, make, revive, adapt and salvage.

The first five actions are about switching-on, while the second five get you more hands-on when you can make time.

Reflect on the role clothes play in your life. Inform yourself about ethical certification and fair trade. Don't be seduced into buying things just because they are on sale. Find more interesting things to do for recreation than shopping. Avoid going to places where you might be tempted to buy things you don't need.

Before you open your money bag, let questions like these pass through your mind:

- Do I need it?
- Do I already have something like it?
- How often will I wear it?
- Will I wear it at least 30 times?[85] #30wears
- Is it well made? Will it last 30 wears?
- Is it easy to care for?

- Does it need dry cleaning?
- Where is it made, and what from?
- Is it a responsible purchase?

Consider supporting social enterprise brands that produce clothes with social justice in mind. Select styles that have multiple uses and fastenings that are flexible with changing waistlines.

NATURAL

My personal preference is to limit synthetics to products that require them, like swimwear and waterproof gear. Synthetic fibres are derived from petroleum and are a type of plastic. Synthetic fibres don't breathe and research shows they are more likely to harbour bacteria and odour than natural fibres.[86] Synthetics also gather static electricity and may cling to your body in uncomfortable and embarrassing ways.

There is no use-by date on simple, natural, well-made clothes.

We can wear them until they wear out.

— Jane Milburn

Reconstituted cellulose fibres—such as viscose, rayon, bamboo, lyocell and tencel—while manmade are derived from plants and wood and therefore more natural then synthetics. They have design advantages, are comfortable to wear and easy care. But there are concerns about chemicals used in their production. Check before you buy using resources such as the Good on You app.[87]

Natural fibres tend to be more expensive and water-intensive to produce, therefore we should treasure them until they literally wear out! Cotton is the dominant natural fibre. Seek out sustainable and organic cotton where you can. Linen is one of the greenest fibres—just machine wash, shake, hang to dry and wear as is. I haven't ironed linen for years—which saves energy and effort (although a short tumble dry gives a nice crinkle). Hemp is less readily available, but equally as green as linen (if not more so). Animal fibres like wool, alpaca, cashmere and silk are expensive and need a little extra care but will last a long time and wear well between washes.

While natural fibre manufacturing is limited in countries like Australia there are groups keen to change that. Full Circle Fibres for example is generating local cotton products.

QUALITY

Buy for the long-term. Quality remains long after the price is forgotten, as the old saying goes. Choose classic styles that will serve you well over time rather than fashion fads. Buy the best you can afford—buy things you love 100 per cent and wear them for a lifetime.

Do your due diligence before handing over cash. Look inside to check seams, finishes, fastenings and fabric type. Brand names may lead to inflated prices, so make sure there is real quality contained within any new purchase rather than smoke and mirrors. Seek out accredited companies that have stood the test of time, or use ethical fashion guides to inform your choices. Use department stores that have ethical sourcing policies, or online options which aggregate brands they trust. Choose brands that have a transparent environmental ethos that encourage recycling and reduced consumption by creating products designed to last a long time.

LOCAL

Since the Rana Plaza tragedy revealed the globalisation race to the bottom on price, ethics and social justice, we have seen a desire to return to localisation. Buy local is a mantra ringing in Australia, in Britain, in America—not just with our clothing but with food and other aspects of life too.

While only a fraction of clothing bought in developed nations is made onshore, there is growing interest in locally-made clothing and footwear. We can foster local industry by spending a little more on items that pay fair wages, and in turn support other local businesses. In Australia for example, Merino Country has set up its own supply chain sourcing wool from New South Wales farms which is processed and made into garments at its factory in Queensland.

A WEARER'S MANIFESTO:

wear clothes, have few,
mostly natural fibres.

— Jane Milburn

Similarly, Rant Clothing uses locally sourced fabric and all clothing production occurs within a 30km radius of its Brisbane studio. In the United States, Alabama Chanin has created local organic cotton fabric specifically for its bespoke clothing range and kits. Many small makers and upcyclers, selling at local markets and online, benefit from a commitment to buy local. You might also like to support local companies that make overseas yet know their supply chains and are Fairtrade-registered.

FEW

Australians have the largest homes in the world followed by United States and Canada: I'm sure this equates to having the biggest wardrobes too! According to Lindsay Wilson from Shrink that Footprint[88], the average new home in Australia is 214m². Compare this to countries with smallest homes: Hong Kong 45m², Russia (57), and the United Kingdom (76).

Minimalists confirm tiny homes and small wardrobes have a lot to recommend them. A portable or capsule wardrobe simplifies our life and choices. While Project 333—having 33 things[89] in your wardrobe for three months—is a global movement, my friend Pam Greet[90] pared her wardrobe down to 50 items (including underwear) in 2016. Minimising her wardrobe maximised her life, Pam maintains.

We can simplify our lives by choosing a signature style and wearing it as a uniform. Perhaps just one style of t-shirt, or one style of dress. Or we may choose one colour and stick with that.

The next five ways to survive and thrive in a material world require more engagement. Are you ready to be hands-on and to make time to be creative?

CARE

Get more life out of what you already own by paying attention and doing running repairs. If you feel a thread snap or notice a seam unravelling, attend to it immediately. As the old saying goes, *a stitch in time saves nine*!

Revaluing the skills of mending does not only extend the life of clothing, it empowers us to create something uniquely individual. Mended garments carry a story of care. They reflect the triumph of imperfection over pretension, while the act of mending itself brings transformation in both mender and mended. By embracing repair

as a valid and useful act, we (the menders) are stitching new life-energy into something others may throw away. When we pause and add a mark of care to our clothes, we extend their life and bring meaning to our own.

It is commonly accepted that up to 25 per cent of the environmental footprint of garments comes from the way we care for them. We can reduce that footprint by caring for clothes in ways that also save us money and time.

Most garments (except coats and jackets) can be hand-washed instead of dry-cleaned, which is a chemical process. 'Dry-clean only' labels are often precautionary, with the key concern being shrinkage.

Wool is particularly vulnerable to moth/silverfish damage. I take a preventive approach by storing wool with cakes of fragrant soap, or sachets of star anise or cloves (sometimes you may have to resort to surface spray, or alternatively store wool in sealed containers). Wash wool with eucalyptus detergent and sponge any food or drink spills. Wool needs less frequent washing than we think. My rule of thumb: unless it smells or looks dirty, don't wash it.

MAKE

Until we make something for ourselves to wear, we cannot appreciate the resources, time and skill that go into the clothes we buy. The fashion industry has conditioned us to be passive consumers. Everyone can buy clothes (with requisite cash or a credit card) yet few know the satisfaction of making something for themselves to wear.

Sewing—or learning to sew—enables us to create something uniquely ours; reflecting our style and personality, independence and creativity. Yet

10 acts of care for clothes (and the environment)

- **nurture attentively** – sponge spills as they happen, restitch dangling button before lost

- **wash less** – only when needed, based on visual inspection and/or sniff test

- **spot clean and freshen** – air them outside or steam with you while showering

- **hand wash delicate items** – use spin cycle to drain excess water and hang to dry

- **choose cold water** – heating water uses most of the electricity required for a wash cycle

- **wash full loads** – even if you adjust the water level, the energy used is the same

- **mix like with like** – check colour-fastness of new purchases, wash fluffy towels with linen

- **use laundry bags and eco-detergents** – help protect delicate items and the ecosystem

- **rest clothes dryers** – use a clothes line or a drying rack, and coat hangers

- **avoid dry-cleaning** – wear special-care clothes for cameo appearances only

Secondhand is the new organic.

When we buy preloved clothes, we do not add chemicals or production stress to the environment. Everything else is various shades of greenwashing.

— Jane Milburn

just because we *can* sew, doesn't mean we do. At group presentations, I usually ask who is wearing something handmade. More often than not, no-one raises a hand.

The reasons given for consuming rather than making include:

- it costs more to sew than to buy readymade, after purchasing fabric, pattern and sewing notions

- after investing time and money in making something, we may be dissatisfied with the outcome

- we need to find space, time and energy to make amid other competing interests.

Yet making things makes us feel good. It may even have measurable mental health benefits, if the applause for baking[91] and knitting[92] is a measure. Working with our hands, head and heart can:

- relieve stress, anxiety and symptoms of depression

- generate a sense of pride and productivity

- enable autonomy and creative choices

- boost brain power through concentration and problem-solving

- slow cognitive decline

- improve motor function.

I'm not advocating we sew *all* our clothes. Rather, that sewing clothes is part of a growing 'maker culture' (think brewing, baking, preserving) because of the satisfaction of doing things for ourselves. A student friend of my daughter was thrilled to tell me she was wearing a skirt she made with her mother, a surgeon. I was equally thrilled for her discovery of how meaningful she had found making a garment with her hands, energy and time—in the hope that more young people may likewise be open to this 'other' way of dressing.

For those who need motivation to stitch again, I offer these suggestions:

- choose simple styles that don't require precise fitting and let the fabric tell the story

- complete your garment before deciding 'it is no good'

- celebrate imperfections in your sewing efforts as chances for creative problem-solving

- be resourceful in sourcing fabric—mix and match what you have, scour op shops for fabric, sheets or tablecloths; fillet clothes you aren't wearing as fabric resources for frills, bindings and pockets

- don't spend money on matching thread—charcoal or cream work with most colours

- buy patterns that you can use multiple times or that include multiple looks (I like KwikSew) or source simple, modern, patterns in your size online (such as Papercut Patterns)

- borrow library books like the *Alabama Stitch Book* which includes beautiful patterns from Natalie Chanin or the many Japanese pattern books

- invest in sewing lessons with someone who shares the love.

REVIVE

Clothing has always been borrowed, exchanged and swapped, through both formal and informal networks. In a climate-changed world, we now have even more reason to embrace clothing revival as a winning strategy.

There is no use-by date on simple, natural, well-made clothes. We can wear them until they wear out. Garments can have second, third, fourth and fifth lifetimes if we keep them in circulation. Landfill is a place of last resort.

Secondhand is the new organic. When we buy preloved clothes, we do not add chemicals or

In the heart of Brisbane, a stiltwalker displays Textile Beat upcycled at Revive 2017.

production stress to the environment. Everything else is various shades of greenwashing.

There are op shops, markets and vintage stores—even the back of your own wardrobes—and then there are clothes swaps with friends and family. A friend has what she calls a 'circular wardrobe', with her sisters and friends passing on garments they no longer wear that still have life and style for another. One maternity outfit was worn during pregnancies of 19 different babies within their network and is still going strong. Obviously they have no problem with preloved.

The secondhand stigma is abating as we seek to develop post-consumerist approaches. Revivalist and futurist style is arising and finely curated by bloggers such as Faye Delanty[93], Hannah Klose[94], Jean Barrett[95], Ellen[96], Leah-Jane Musch[97] and Jonathan Pampling[98] to name a few.

An additional benefit of wearing preloved clothes is reduced stress. You don't have to worry about your clothes so much since you haven't invested a fortune in them.

Let's put fresh thinking into why it pays to op shop:

• The garments you purchase have inherent ethical and sustainable values, regardless of their origin.

• You don't extract virgin resources from Earth and are part of the solution by reusing existing ones.

• It is a great way to experiment with your style by trying colours and shapes not available as 'new'.

• You never feel under pressure to make a purchase and can inspect garments at your leisure.

• Older garments are often better-made than new ones, and chemical residues already washed out.

• The money you save by not buying new can be deployed to holidays or supporting those in need.

• Spending money in local op shops supports the good work of charities in communities.

My ten top tips for op shopping

1. Location – visit affluent suburbs or regional areas where there's better choice and less competition.

2. Seek out smaller, church-run op shops that are less formally curated and managed.

3. Pop in regularly – good treasure is quickly snapped up.

4. Buy only quality items, preferably made from natural materials.

5. Check all quarters – scan for appealing colours, textures and shapes in every section.

6. Think creatively about what you see and how it might be repurposed.

7. Invest time – search to the bottom of piles and bins for overlooked treasure.

8. Get to know the volunteers and staff – know when sales and special deals are on.

9. Go casual – wear comfy clothes for quick try-ons and plan a route to visit several in one outing.

10. When you get home, wash or sponge everything to freshen it up and make it your own.

ADAPT

The most creative and playful way to survive and thrive in a material world is to adapt existing clothing to suit yourself—upcycle garments already in circulation to create something new from old.

At a time when poor quality throwaway clothing is at its zenith, redesign and refashion are the ultimate expressions of Slow Clothing. Taking time to slice and dice unworn garments, then collage and stitch them together into a new form, creates something unique in the world.

Upcycling appeals on many levels because it is useful, resourceful and playful. Most people get the message about consumption overload, yet few personally invest energy and time in turning the tide. When we do, the results reflect our true selves and provide ultimate satisfaction.

Upcycling is a way to revive home sewing in the 21st century. Sewing becomes empowering and ethical. Instead of sewing from scratch, existing resources can be recreated to suit yourself and reduce waste. Anything old can be new again when we have the skills and willingness to invest the time. Indeed, think of fibre and clothing as material resources and focus on refreshing, reusing and recycling—doing good for ourselves and the environment.

If you are not interested in upcycling for yourself, you can seek out specialised upcycling businesses such as those being pioneered by local creatives (in Australia these include Spunky Bruiser in Sydney and Gathered Pieces in Melbourne). In their book *Junky Styling*, veteran UK upcyclers Sanders and Seager said:

> Recycling worn, discarded, second-hand clothing involves taking a garment that already has an identity and looking at it as a raw material, studying the existing form and details, then applying them to a new design—a

Seven fabulous attributes of upcycling

- **creative** – we learn through play, see mistakes as opportunities to problem solve

- **individual** – we use imagination, be unique, take risks, be disruptive and non-conformist

- **limitless** – upcycling is an ongoing process, using natural fibres until they wear out

- **mindful** – thoughtful focus on the task at hand, with a sense of purpose and achievement in making

- **empowering** – we create our own style that suits our shape and needs

- **ethical** – not exploiting people or resources, truly green, save money for worthy purposes

- **connected** – we develop an emotional bond to clothes we have cared for or created

Granny Edna Milburn's rag rug, made in 1993.

complete reinterpretation and disregard for the existing identity of the piece. This involves a vision and an understanding of form and functionality. We reckon that you can recycle anything, and it's a wonderful way to engage our imaginations. With such a vast array of materials used in clothing, we have always maintained that distinction between 'natural' and 'manmade' fabric. The quality of natural textiles has always made them first choice for our raw materials.

I have a commitment to endless upcycling therefore my wardrobe is always a work in progress. It is the fabrics, textures and colours— rather than the current design—that influence my preferences.

When we adopt an upcycling mindset, we instinctively restyle, restitch or recreate what is around us, rather than buying new. There are simple refashion ideas to consider in Chapter 5.

SALVAGE

There are endless opportunities to repurpose cloth when we turn our minds to it. The list below presents just a few options to get you thinking:

Cleaning cloths: There's something quite lovely about seeing a favourite old sheet or garment turn up in your cleaning rags. Memories resurface of what that piece of cloth used to be. Resourceful people turn worn-out clothing into cleaning rags, or put natural-fibres into the compost.

Creative reuse of t-shirts.

hemming was not required). T-shirts can become eco-shopping bags, eco-jewellery or knitting yarn. Shirts can become cushion covers or frills on a skirt. Denim from jeans is robust and has an extraordinary array of upcycling potential including bags, bunting, carriers and containers.

Useful remnant pieces of fabric are also being repurposed into replacements for plastic shopping bags through the community initiative of Boomerang Bags.[99]

Threads of change

Change takes time. There is no pressure to adopt all these actions into our busy lives. It is more a case of starting easy and doing *something*. Learning to stitch is enough!

Slow Clothing is an evolutionary concept, a journey of discovery stepping back from the high consumption treadmill. It is about creating and wearing your own style, and ensuring it doesn't cost the Earth. Have fun being bold and creative, as you learn to survive, and thrive, in a material world.

Start here

- Become conscious of what you are wearing – appreciate your clothes like friends
- Think before you spend any money – make ethical choices that don't cost the Earth
- Have a goal to buy well and less often – wear your clothes for longer to reduce waste

Compost: When natural-fibre garments wear out, they effectively biodegrade and return organic matter to the soil. Be aware the thread in the seams will generally be polyester, so you may want to cut this away before adding the cloth to the compost or using it as groundcover under bark mulch.

Handmade eco-products: The eco-statement of imperfect yet handmade upcycled products need to be valued for their authenticity and sincerity, rather than matching the latest design aesthetic. Old clothes and linen can be upcycled into an endless array of accessories and homewares, including quilts, rag rugs and wall hangings. I recently turned my children's long outgrown hand-painted t-shirts into soft and personal hankies (knit doesn't fray, so

When we follow a pattern,

we create something in another's shadow. When we explore our own creativity, something original emerges.

— Jane Milburn

Chapter 5 AUTONOMY

Simple DIY techniques
Stitch, mend and upcycle

It is empowering to become more self-sufficient and independent. Before buying anything new, revisit what is already available and see what can be done to make it work better for you.

Upcycling is fun! Give yourself permission to play, to develop your creativity and live directly in the world. We learn by doing. We all say 'I don't have time' and certainly there are stages of life when that is true. Making time for upcycling is part of the challenge of Slow Clothing and sometimes it means letting go of the need to 'keep up'.

The upcycling techniques I share are freeform and unconventional, and are unlikely to suit people who prefer order and neatness. Upcycling, by its nature, requires us to suspend ideas of perfection because we are working with materials that are not consistent or homogenous. We don't live in a perfect world, so why do we expect ourselves and our clothes to be so?

Embrace imperfection. Being perfect is impossible to maintain. Dysfunctional or discarded clothes

provide opportunities for experimentation and learning new skills in ways that cost little. The potential for upcycling is endless, limited only by imagination, and available time and skills. Remember that Slow Clothing is about individual expression and personal connection to what we wear. We stitch to make a mark and be mindful. We are original, natural and resourceful.

Tradition and convention tend to lock us into established beliefs. At one time, cutting up garments was discouraged but times have changed and dysfunctional clothing is fair game. A jumper is a jumper—until we turn it upside down and it becomes a skirt! Make a little time and space, gather resources (old clothes, linens, fabric from op shops) in appealing textures and colours. Don't overdo it, or you may be overwhelmed.

Many people upcycle clothing into homewares— bags, pouches, quilts, cushions and curtains. With the tips and tricks on the following pages, we are taking it a step further and creating garments for ourselves to wear.

Basic tools

- pins and safety pins
- pin cushion
- scissors – fabric scissors and thread snips
- needles – some with large eyes
- threads – including crochet and cottons for decorative stitching
- tape measure
- sewing machine – nothing fancy required
- optional extras: an iron, a mannequin, an over-locker

Handstitching

Hand-stitching has much to recommend it and enables you to make small changes to garments. When you relax into it, you can enjoy the therapeutic benefits with every stitch. Another huge benefit is portability, you can take hand-stitching with you anywhere.

We can stitch in whatever way we want and all the better if it looks a little imperfect, announcing it as handmade not machine-made. The only thing that matters is knotting on and knotting off, so that it is robust enough to survive many wash and wear cycles. Cut a piece of thread that is about 80cm long. Use a single thread until confident as sometimes a double thread is prone to extra knotting.

Knotting on

There are many ways to knot on. I remember Mum showing me to wrap the tail end once around my index finger and roll it off to form the knot.

Another way, known as a quilters knot, is shown in these four diagrams. Start with a large thread and needle, so you can clearly see the process. This is a knot you will use for a lifetime.

1. Thread the needle, position the tail end of the thread along your index finger and place the needle down on top with two-thirds of it (the needle) sitting beyond the thread.

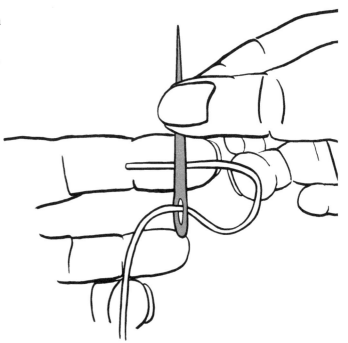

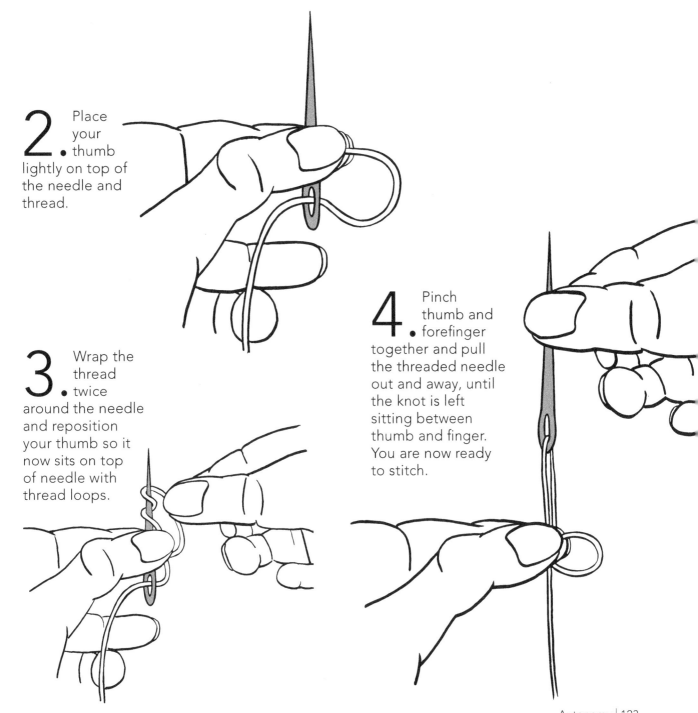

2. Place your thumb lightly on top of the needle and thread.

3. Wrap the thread twice around the needle and reposition your thumb so it now sits on top of needle with thread loops.

4. Pinch thumb and forefinger together and pull the threaded needle out and away, until the knot is left sitting between thumb and finger. You are now ready to stitch.

Running stitch

Running stitch is the most versatile hand stitch and simply involves movement of the needle and thread from one side of the fabric to the other with progression to form a row of stitches.

Once the needle is threaded and knotted, as per previous page, you insert it from the back or inside of the work, and pull it through to the front. You may want to do individual stitches from back to front while you settle into the work. When ready, you can load up the needle by pointing it in and out a few times, then pull the thread through in one go. You may need to adjust the tension so the stitches lie flat against the fabric (unless you want it gathered slightly for some reason). When you load up the needle, aim to push the fabric on to the needle, rather than push the needle through the fabric. Make sure your stitches are about 1cm or less in length so they don't get caught on things. If a loop knot appears mid-thread as you are stitching, insert the tip of your needle in the loop and jerk the loop away from the knot and it should untangle. As you become more proficient, you can start with a backstitch (a stitch that goes back on itself) rather than a knot.

Knotting off

After a run of stitching, ensure you have about 5-10cm of thread (as a beginner, less when you know how) left on your needle to begin the knotting off process. It is useful to do one tight little stitch to secure the tension of your work before you knot off as described in these diagrams.

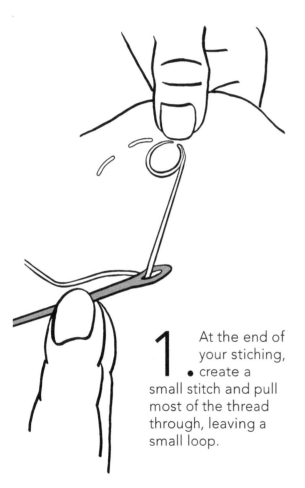

1. At the end of your stiching, create a small stitch and pull most of the thread through, leaving a small loop.

2. Pass your needle through this loop and pull most of the thread through it.

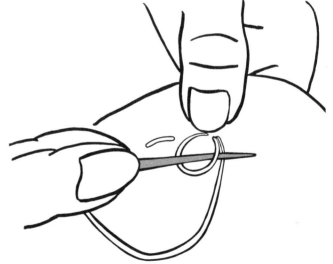

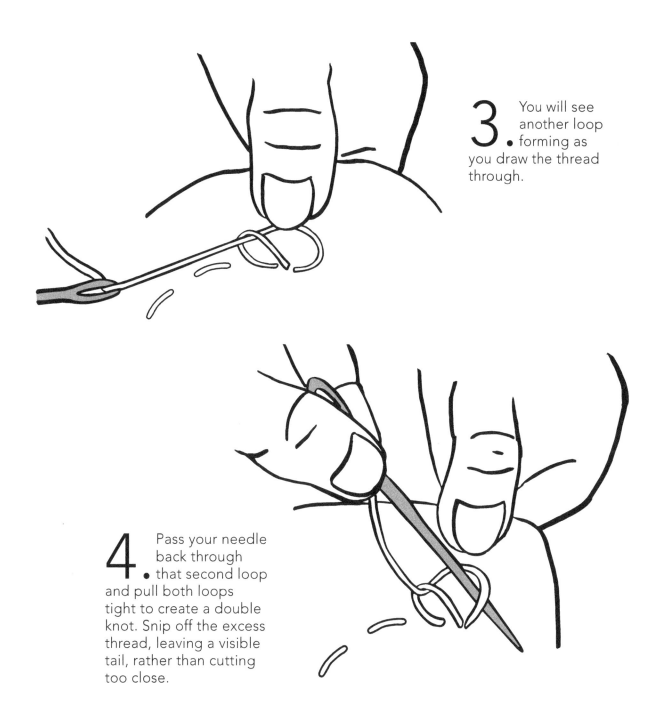

3. You will see another loop forming as you draw the thread through.

4. Pass your needle back through that second loop and pull both loops tight to create a double knot. Snip off the excess thread, leaving a visible tail, rather than cutting too close.

Star stitch

Start from the back, form one running stitch, then work your way around in a circular motion. You may find it helpful to mark the first few stars with chalk to guide your way. This is a useful stitch for decoration and in what is known as kantha or boro stitching techniques where layers are being added to reinforce worn fabrics.

Blanket stitch

This is useful for finishing cut edges, or to add detail and decoration to plain garments. The hardest part is starting! Begin from behind, bringing needle out through the edge of the fabric, then work from the front by inserting needle to the back and bringing it up to pass through the loop as it forms.

Cross stitch

There are several ways to form the crosses, whatever works for you is good. You can form each cross individually, or do them in a run by making parallel stitches one way then come back across the other way.

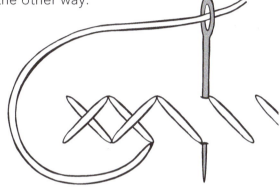

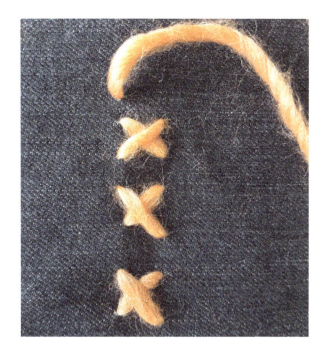

T stitch

Bring thread up from the back, create one stitch then put needle to the back and position it to come up in the opposite quarter to form another stitch that creates a t-shape. Alternatively, do one row of stitches one way, and another row perpendicular to it.

Feather Stitch

A decorative stitch to enhance or embellish plain surfaces or define edges. While it might look complicated, it is just wielding the needle in such a way that the thread loops around the needle and is caught by the stitch.

Satin Stitch

Close and continuous stitching mainly used for decorative effect to embellish plain fabric or disguise fabric flaws, holes or stains.

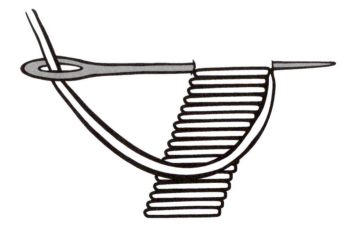

Darning

Darning is a way to repair holes in fabric. Essentially, you need to replace the fabric by weaving new threads (a weft and a warp). Using knitting wool or another substantial thread, make long stitches across the hole (check tension to avoid puckering) then change to the opposite direction and weave in and out of these threads to fill the hole. It may help to use a wooden darning mushroom or substitute (drink bottle or orange) to keep the darning surface smooth. If you are darning a sock, avoid using knots by weaving the ends back on themselves. If the hole is very small, just make one stitch left to right and another top to bottom.

Darning can be decorative using contrasting or multi-coloured threads to please your eye. Subsequent wearing of the socks will mean the threads felt together. Ensure you darn into the fabric beyond the physical hole as it currently exists, to prempt future weaknesses there.

Sew on a button

Anyway you attach a button is a good way. The method shown here enables a neat finish, if that is what you prefer. Note: You can position a toothpick at the back of garment, so the stitches go over it. When removed, this enables a taller stalk to be created as might be required for a thick coat.

1. Knot on and align your knot so it will sit beneath the button (on front side of garment). Place your button down over the knot.

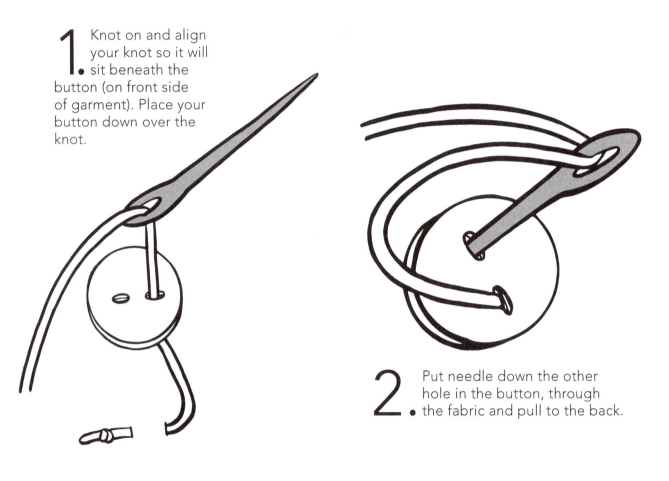

2. Put needle down the other hole in the button, through the fabric and pull to the back.

3. Proceed to put the needle back up and down through the button holes (about four to six times).

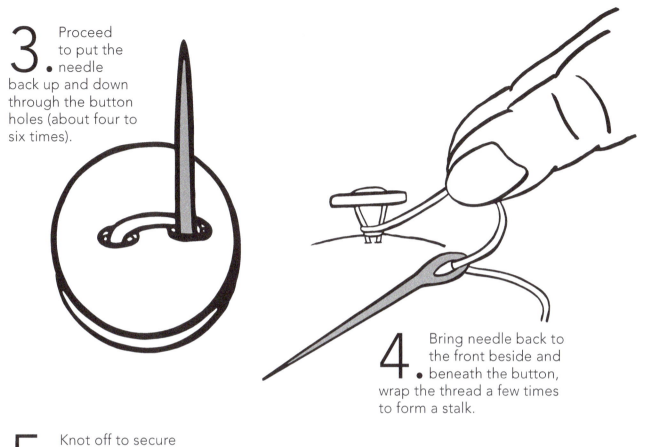

4. Bring needle back to the front beside and beneath the button, wrap the thread a few times to form a stalk.

5. Knot off to secure and snip excess thread.

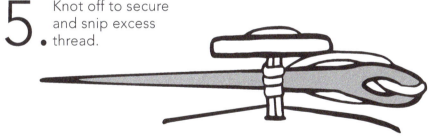

Patching

There is no limit as to what can be done with hand-stitching to repair and embellish garments. Use an old t-shirt or wool garment to create your patches, which can then be applied from above, or below (cut away the top layer after you have attached the patch underneath). Use running stitch and decorate with buttons or threads, to your own style. Note: for an even-shaped heart patch, fold the fabric along vertical midline and cut both sides at once.

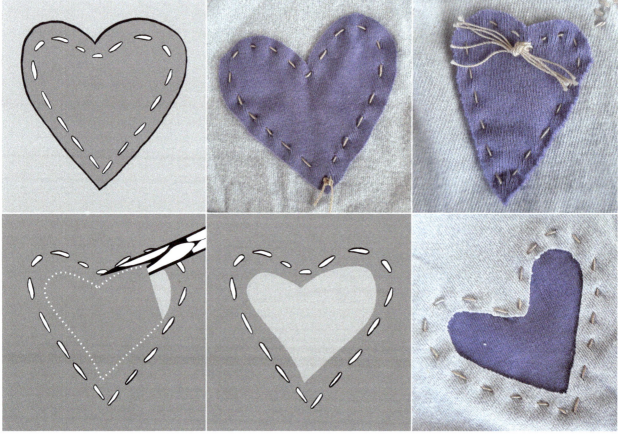

Embellishing

Apply your creativity to decorate plain fabric or cover stains. You can also adapt ill-fitting sleeves, collars, or areas where fabric has been eroded (by insects or wear).

You may find it useful to embellish kilt pins or cover button badges to become brooches. These are multi-purpose as fasteners or simply for decorative effect.

Sewing pouch

Cut the bottom 22cm off a jeans leg, turn inside out, stitch across the cut edge, then square off each corner about 3cm from each side. Turn right side out. Use a 60cm length of t-shirt ribbon or other, stitch in middle to one side near the original hemline of jean (which becomes top of pouch). Note: to make t-shirt ribbon, cut 1cm wide strips, then pull each end so they roll-up.

Notebook cover

Find a standard notebook (about 15 x 21cm) which you can replace when full. Open notebook and place upon a flat piece of jean leg cut to about 23 x 52 cm. Mark where the front pocket will sit and stitch in place at this point. Open book, on inside of denim, and wrap denim at both ends to form a 'book cover'. Pin top and bottom edges, remove book, stitch across top and bottom and fringe edges.

Make sewing resources

If you are just starting on your upcycling and sewing journey, you can make a few resources out of old denim. I prefer a naive style that embraces imperfection and shows the previous life of textiles. If you are making by hand, there's nothing wrong with looking hand-hewn. Use some old well-worn denim jeans, your own or from the op shop. Explore your creativity by playing with pieces, guided by the simple instructions on facing and following pages. Follow your own instincts, curiosity and problem-solving abilities if required.

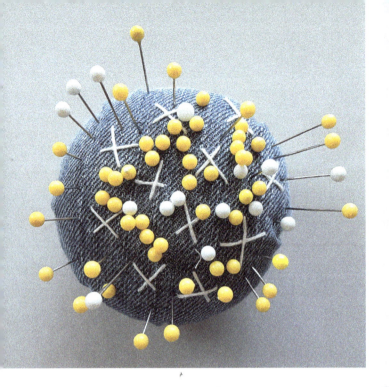

Pin cushion

Think about this as creating a cushion with an insert. For the insert, cut two smaller circles (about 12cm diameter), stuff and secure. For outside, cut one bigger circle (17cm diameter) and pull this together around the insert (do running stitch around the outside of the big circle, pull up and secure with stitching). Cover the opening by stitching on a small square of fabric. This particular style was shown to me by Akiko Ike in Japan, who uses spent coffee grounds as stuffing, and I have used sand.

Needle book

Cut a piece of denim from jean leg (about 20 x 15cm) and a piece of cotton wadding, old towel or similar (8 x 15cm). Fold up 1/3 of longest edge (20cm) of denim piece to form a pouch, pin at outer edge, then stitch wadding across the middle (to create a book). Use running stitch to secure outer edges of pouch and decorate outside with button or other.

Creative upcycling

Every garment is different and I encourage you to follow your own instincts and creativity to achieve unique outcomes. I also hope you complete and wear each garment you upcycle. The learning is in the doing, and the wearing. It is too easy to criticise ourselves and our efforts: too easy to get partway through and abandon because it is not looking good at one point. Yet when we embrace each imperfect effort, we move further along the continuum to expertise.

The instructions that follow are not a full step-by-step process and assume some understanding of basic sewing principles. If you are a complete beginner, or uncertain on some cutting or sewing details, link up with someone more experienced who is prepared to apply their skills in an adventurous way. If you have no-one to help, seek out online resources, or buy a commercial pattern for a simple knit skirt and/or shift and extrapolate their instructions. You could also borrow library books that includes patterns, or attend an upcycling workshop.

I have included some pattern outlines to show the way I upcycle. They will be a guide only, based on my own shape which is Size 10-12 (hips – 106cm, waist – 80cm, bust – 88cm, and height of 157cm) and seam allowance is included. I like my clothes loose-fitting to allow for weight fluctuations. Check your measurements against those indicated here, and add or subtract width as needed from the centre-fold or midline in each case. I use old sheets to cut out my pattern shapes because cotton is more robust and easier to work with than paper. A seam allowance is included.

A good way to start upcycling is to choose something that fits your upper body, and tweak the extremities—the collar, sleeves and skirt. This dress, left, is made from items gathered from op shops in a small Western Australian town, upcycled using handstitch only. It began as a white dress with puffy sleeves, which I cut off and made into pockets. A handmade linen doily forms the front collar, the centre of a tablecloth the back collar, while the rest of that tablecloth is added as a hankerchief hemline. Additional linen pieces are added for length and decorative effect.

Upcycled collars

Revive and revitalise tired shirts, tops and dresses by changing the collar line. This may involve cutting off the old formal, worn or stained collar and adding a new, more relaxed replacement or simply turning over once (or twice) and hand-stitching to finish. If the shirt has a buttoned front, think about where the first button will sit in relation to the new collar before making the cut. Create new collars by estimating length required, cutting a fabric remnant on the bias (diagonally across the straight grain) and attaching by machine or handstitch to the neckline. Doilies and scarves may also prove useful. These photos give you some ideas. The fringed collar, above left, once was a shirt that I cut into strips on the bias then machine-stitched to the neckline of a dress. The bottom of one sleeve serves as a phone pouch.

Long loose skirt to summer dress

You know those gorgeous long skirts that once were fashionable? We can turn them into cool summer dresses with just the slightest of tweaks. The body circumference under your arms will most likely be equal to or less than the circumference of your waist—you may already know this from wearing elastic-waist skirts as strapless dresses.

Here are some suggestions:

1. Find similar or contrasting strips of fabric (potentially from old garments, it doesn't need to be new fabric). When these are attached to the front and back of a skirt waistband, it becomes a dress. You can attach the straps using decorative hand-stitching, buttons or even safety pins! Consider crossing straps over, tying bows or knotting them for interest. An upcycled dress using this technique can be found at sewitagain.com (Sew 36).

2. If your skirt has a drawstring and/or elastic waist, you can undo part of one side seam to become an armhole and turn it into a one-shoulder dress. Begin your unpicking just below the waist band and continue for about 22cm, enough to be a comfortable but not revealing armhole. An upcycled dress using this technique can be found at sewitagain.com (Sew 40).

3. If you are ready for a little more sewing, you can turn a full skirt with a narrow waistband into a cool strappy shift, by cutting out D shapes just below the waistband and using bias binding to finish these cut edges. (See white skirt dress, at right, which is Sew 42 on sewitagain.com).

4. And if you are really adventurous, you can tilt the skirt on its side to become a swing top by opening up part of the side seam (begin midway down one side and open just enough to go over the head) to become the neckline. The old waistline becomes one sleeve, while the old hemline can be fastened (with a safety pin or hand-stitches) to create the other sleeve. Best worn over tights and t-shirt. An upcycled dress using this technique can be found at sewitagain.com (Sew 279).

Photo by Tim Swinson, as published in Ruth Magazine by the Queensland Country Women's Association.

Jumper skirts

Transforming old reject jumpers/sweaters into skirts is a favourite and easy upcycle. The jumper needs to fit over your hips and there are at least two ways to transform it. The skirt pattern guide gives you an indication of the shape you are aiming for, based on your own hip circumference (add more or less down the midline).

Upside jumper skirt

The hem of the jumper becomes the hem of the skirt. Turn the jumper inside out, cut off the sleeves to use for the shrug or beanie as you wish. Leave most of the existing jumper side seams in place, and trim the upper edges into the skirt shape. You are likely to need a thin piece of elastic (cut to your waist measurement) and you can make a casing using one of three methods. With each method, you leave a small opening to thread the elastic through using a safety pin then secure both ends together (unless you are familiar with stitching-in an elastic circle).

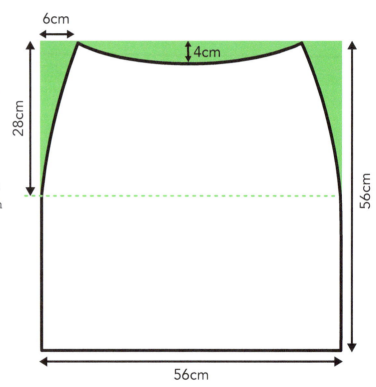

- Turn over 1cm seam at top of skirt and stitch down by hand or with machine.

- Sew bias binding along the cut edge and turn inside to form an elastic casing.

- Add a stretch fabric band, that can also serve to lengthen the jumper skirt, and place the elastic in this band.

Upside-down jumper skirt

With this method, the hem of the jumper or cardigan becomes the waist of the skirt. The 'new' waist may feel secure without elastic, otherwise use one of methods on previous page to add elastic. Alternatively simply thread hat elastic on a large-eyed needle through the waist line and pull-up to required tightness. Cut off the bottom half of each sleeve and set aside for other projects, or turn into a phone pouch or beanie. Cut along the top of the remaining part of each sleeve and through the shoulder seams to open up the new hemline of your skirt. Edge with handstitch, zig zag on the sewing machine, or trim with fabric.

The cut-open sleeve falls interestingly and provides movement when you walk. Can be trimmed to a more curved shape if preferred.

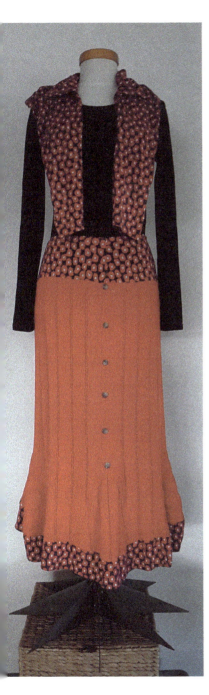

Pinny shift dress

This is a dress without darts or openings, which drops over your head in a loose and comfortable style. It is designed to be worn with a camisole, t-shirt or skivvy underneath which are easily washed, so the pinny itself only needs an occasional wash between airing and wearing.

The pinny is a method I use to reform old garments including jeans, linens or suits. You can either find a shift dress pattern that works for you, cut one off an existing shift you own (remembering to add 1cm seam allowance where it is needed) or you can extrapolate this pattern which includes seam allowance.

Once the pattern is sorted, you make a front and a back, then stitch these together at the shoulder and side seam. You will most likely want to make the back neck higher than the front neck, you can cut an extra piece and pin it on the pattern or just make this adjustment organically.

To make the pinny, lay your pattern on a table, then place pieces on top so they overlap at least one centimetre. When you have the pattern covered, pin the pieces in place (careful to avoid pinning to the pattern underneath), then carefully lift this body piece to the sewing machine and topstitch in place (working from the neckline to the hem when possible).

There are several things to consider: place your fabric pieces so you do not end up trying to

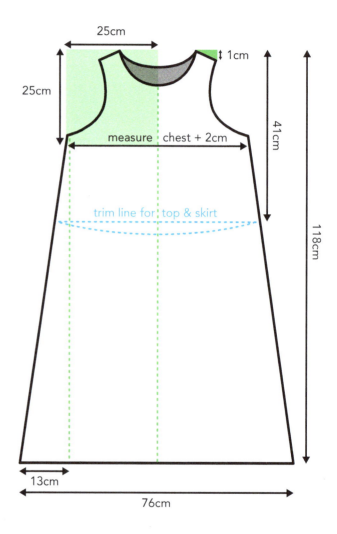

topstitch two chunky bits (ie bands of jeans) or have them abutting each other when you sew the front to the back side.

History Skirt

These skirts are made by creating panels of texture, which are stitched together to form a circle skirt that it topped with a band of knit fabric and elastic waistband. The hemline is trimmed with a double layer of woven fabric.

Gather various pieces of fabric or old clothing in colours you like. Cut 5-8 skirt panels (five panels for small, eight for large) in similar-weight fabric. Embellish these panels with pockets, buttons, lace, flowers etc (keep any thick layers away from what will be the seams of each panel). Arrange the completed panels in a circle on your work table or floor, move them around until they are balanced to your eye. Pin panel sides together into a circle skirt formation then stitch together. Form your length of knit fabric into a circle and attach as a waistband. Add the hem trim and further embellish the panels if required.

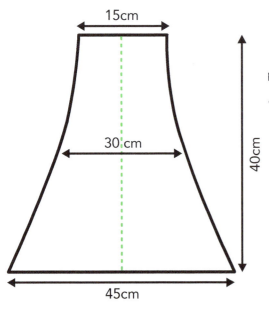

Pattern for one panel of a history skirt, which is a collage of panels (the number depends on circumference needed for your size) sewn together to form a circle then finished with stretch knit waist band and fabric trimmed hem.

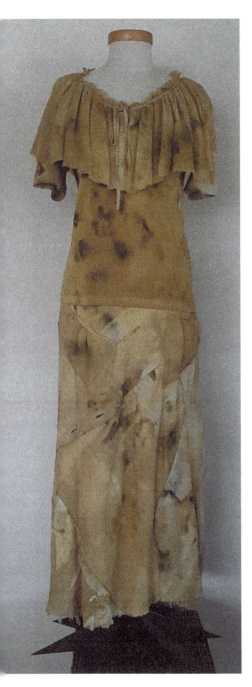

Ecodye

Dyeing clothes with plants is about experimentation. It is a great way to transform, unify, or grunge-up disparate garments that can then be worn as they are, or restitched together in creative ways. At the very least, a stained or dull garment will get a new life when it has been through a dye transformation process.

If you have to, you can start with a cooking pot on your kitchen stove providing there is good ventilation and you wash the pot well if later using for cooking. Better to use old pots outside. I have a couple of large old pots, a table and a portable gas burner near the laundry, and periodically make time for a dyeing spree.

At its simplest the process is to add colour-making vegetation to the pot, cover it with water and boil for about an hour to extract colour. Turn heat to simmer and remove the vegetation. Drop your prepared garment in the dyebath with heat on very low, leave it for 30 minutes to one hour, then turn the heat off. You can remove and unwrap your garment at this point, but I prefer to leave it in the brew overnight to cool and maximize the extraction of colour and creation of marks.

Protein fibres (silk and wool) absorb colour much easier than plant fibres (cotton and linen). Adding a mordant helps fix the colour. Small rusty pieces of iron (rusty nails and washers, tools, chain) added to the dye bath, or wrapped within the garment, is an easy way to include an iron mordant and keep the colours dark. Aluminium sulphate is another mordant I have used but it brings out more yellow tones.

Although you can just drop the garment in the dyepot, I usually wrap it up with string. Lay the garment on a flat surface, arrange some leaves (eg Eucalyptus), petals, dry tea leaves, onion skins, tumeric, purple carrot slices and rusty tools on it. Sprinkle over some of the prepared dye water to moisten the garment, fold up then tie it with string (like a rolled pot roast). The leaves etc need to be closely touching the fabric to create marks on the fabric surface.

Bark creates great browns and rusty reds. Ironbark and various other barks are useful, and can be soaked in a bucket to help draw out the colour. Soaking leaves for months also helps release colour and prints. If you loved playing mud-pies as a child, ecodyeing enables you to revisit that as a adult. Experiment on your own or learn from reference books such as India Flint's, *Eco colour* and *Second Skin*.

Opshopchop coat

This technique is what I call opshopchop. It is a coat created from a jumper, a cardigan and a scarf, that began life as different neutral-coloured wool garments that went through the dyepot and were then cut and sewn for a fresh life. It is best to make this by draping on a mannequin, but a patient and willing friend would do!

The jumper (cut off-centre up the front) forms the base structure for this garment. One arm of the cardigan is cut off to replace an arm on the jumper. The other cardigan sleeve is cut open (from underside) and the cardigan turned upside down and positioned from across the front, then wraps (on the diagonal) across the back of the jumper and around to the front again where it is attached to the base of the jumper. Once the cardigan is secured across the back, the excess jumper (sitting under the cardigan) can be cut off and redeployed to elongate the jumper at the front. The scarf is attached from the front collar, to drape around the back neck and be attached along the front cut edge of the jumper. I used some offcuts to decorate a nappy pin which secures the garment at the front. It is worn over an eco-dyed wool shirt, and a skirt made from other cut-up garments using a long version of the skirt pattern shown earlier.

Ten ways stitching enhances life

1. Expands choice – not restricted by what you can find ready made

2. Provides agency – everyone's body is different, it is great to be able to suit yourself

3. Offers challenge – how can I make this work?

4. Enables repair – extend life of favourite garments

5. Gives a sense of accomplishment – gain real achievement from completing tasks and details

6. Encourages creativity – grown up play

7. Connects us with clothing – we put energy and care into a garment we make or repair for ourselves.

8. Creates mindful immersion – through soothing repetitive actions

9. Saves unnecessary expenditure

10. Reduces waste

In the rush to own things for reasons of status and looks, we lose the opportunity to be mindful and resourceful through the act of making and creating.

— Jane Milburn

Chapter 6 REFLECTIONS

Because we care
What people have said and what the future holds

Never at any time in history have there been so many clothes in wardrobes of the world and through a process of exploration and analysis, I have navigated a way to make sense of that.

This rethinking of clothing culture is grounded in everyday practice. We are now having conversations about the substance of clothing in a sustainability and lifestyle context—alongside local food, soul craft, and composting—instead of just fashionable looks and styles.

Slow Clothing is part of emergent thinking around revaluing material things, as articulated by economist Richard Denniss in *Curing Affluenza: How to buy less stuff and save the world*. Similarly, it taps into the return to a making and repairing culture documented by Katherine Wilson in *Tinkering: Australians reinvent DIY culture*.

I've shared with many the simple pleasure of tinkering with our clothes to make them last longer and negate the need for buying more. This tinkering develops our curiosity and creativity as it builds resilience and independence from the earn more to spend more consumer cycle. Many people and groups have provided input and opportunities to share these engaged ways of dressing and some of their feedback appears on the following pages. It has been personally satisfying to see the uptake of upcycling as a conscious practice, with many young people interested in its potential for customising their clothes.

Going forward, we need to bring creative reuse into sustainability teaching and nurture local natural fibre systems. We also need to support the re-emerging maker culture and reskill ourselves and future generations for doing running repairs (as a minimum).

What we choose to wear shows who we are and what we believe in. I will continue championing Slow Clothing and natural fibres by travelling, writing and developing more resources to shine light on ways we can live creatively and sustainably, and within our means.

Brisbane's waste minimisation efforts form part of our holistic approach to making our city the cleanest, greenest and most sustainable city in Australia. In striving toward truly sustainable practices, it's important to recognise that Recycling does not sit at the top of the waste hierarchy. Above it are the preferred options to Avoid, Reduce, Reuse and Repair items. When it comes to effectively addressing the growing problem of textile waste, all of these preferences are particularly relevant.

Jane Milburn's enthusiasm and passion to reduce textile waste has highlighted to the community how easy it is to incorporate textile reuse and repair skills into our everyday lives. In doing so, she has facilitated a cultural shift for many residents to reconsider their purchasing behaviours and the value they place on textiles. Jane's advocacy and collaborative approach with Brisbane City Council ultimately led to the establishment of Council's Revive Second-hand Fashion Festival, an event which has grown into a highly anticipated feature in our city's civic calendar. Each year, thousands of residents participate in Revive and we are honoured to have collaborated with Jane in a way that both raises awareness and celebrates how far we've come as a city.

Cr Peter Matic
Chairman, Field Services Committee, Brisbane City Council, Queensland

The Home Economics Institute of Australia (HEIA) connected with Jane Milburn in August 2014 and her subsequent workshop at the 2015 HEIA Queensland conference received rave reviews. Since then, Jane has presented at many HEIA events, regionally and interstate, and was a keynote speaker at the HEIA 2017 national conference in Melbourne.

Jane's textile message has been consistent, but each time she added twists and turns to make us think and act more deeply, more critically and more creatively. Across our journeys with Jane, members of HEIA have had the opportunity to explore The upcycled way, Refashioning, A time for Slow Clothing, Valuing old skills in a new world, and A change of clothes. The exploration has been one of great learning, of having lots of fun and of being totally inspired. The following comments from delegates at workshops and conferences sum up Jane's impact:

- Great practical experience, awesome ideas and creations.
- Excellent. Inspirational. Wonderful engaging presenter.
- Great PD. So much knowledge given from Jane.
- Informative, innovative and provocative
- Inspirational—love the whole sustainability idea.
- Hands on skills. Participants had projects to work on.
- So many different ideas and techniques shown.
- This was good fun that was had during serious discussions about this issue.
- Jane's passion and expertise were an inspiration.
- I will never look at a T-shirt or denims in the same way, knowing that I can create a new article.
- How inspiring is that woman!!
- This was phenomenal, so inspiring.
- An excellent presentation that highlighted the need to think of clothing as more than just fashion.

Thank you, Jane, for being an excellent and inspirational tour guide on our journeys. We haven't reached our destination yet but we have travelled to places we have never been before. These places have touched our hearts, our minds, and our creative and ethical spirits. We are inspired to not only contribute to planetary health through our fashion and textile practices, but also to take the young people in our classrooms on a similar journey whilst also having fun and being creative.

Dr Janet Reynolds
HEIA(Q) Professional Development and Conference Convenor, Queensland

Photo by Shellie Buckle.

My fibre upcycling journey began with my grandmothers. Great women with whom I always had fun making clothes, mending, knitting, crocheting and using leftover fabric for other garments and dolls clothes. We created for enjoyment and to value materials. Into my late teen days at college, I discovered op shopping and upcycled garments of any size I fell in love with by adding side panels to dresses and cutting off sleeves.

Later in life a turning point happened when Cath Jarvis organised a Textile Beat upcycling workshop, introducing Jane Milburn to our lives. I had read of Jane's work shining a light on natural fibres and raising awareness of petro-chemical fabric consumption and waste. Being a wool grower who chooses to wear only wool and cotton, plus enjoying making for meaning, I decided I just had to attend this two-day workshop and packed a suitcase with clothes I had upcycled as the brochure stated a 'share and tell' session was included. I arrived an hour late (long story), burst in the door carrying suitcase and sewing machine, and remember being introduced to all and Jane said 'Welcome, so glad you travelled three hours, I'd love for you to show us your treasures in the suitcase'. Two days spent with Jane inspiring us with upcycling tips, dyeing fibres, insightful conversations on consumption, generous sharing of ideas for creativity; this was Jane revealing leadership knowledge.

That session opened a door for me to journey forth and the next year I organised our library to host a two-day Textile Beat workshop coordinated with the annual Waste to Art Competition. This opportunity reached out to many people, including an afternoon workshop with school children, and they all embraced it. I wanted to give my community the opportunity to meet Jane, to be encouraged by her, to hear her conversation of how we can rethink the idea of fashion, fabric, fibre and be more aware of the sustainability issues behind our consumption.

We who are passionate about upcycling, not only clothes but everything that can be reused and repurposed, all have a story. The story for me is about the value of having skills and sharing them. Thank you Jane for championing the cause.

Elly Tom, farmer and grazier
'Carinya', Parkes, New South Wales

Jane envisaged her Slow Clothing work when undertaking a Graduate Certificate of Australian Rural Leadership, which was established through a partnership between James Cook University and the Australian Rural Leadership Foundation. Her final assignment required a plan identifying both theoretical and practical elements of her future leadership. Her Slow Clothing plan touched upon multiple layers of our modern lifestyle and causes us to question our relationship with the environment; our capitalist society, consumerism and the commercialisation of goods; our relationships with people and materials; our sense of place; and our treatment of time and space. Jane has followed through with her plan and created a pathway to living that should make us all rethink our current trajectory into the future. She is constantly building upon and increasing her complexity of understanding of clothing and natural fibres, drawing solidly from practices of the past. In sharing this, she brings people together to really appreciate and practice not just the remaking of clothing but the remaking of how we want to live our lives.

Dr Jennifer Andrew, Canberra, Australian Capital Territory

Our journey began by forging connections through the Australian Rural Leadership program with those synergies for care and concern for regional Australia. During a leadership exercise designed to encourage deeper reflection of oneself and the discovery of one's potential, Jane honed her leadership direction. This leadership chapter embraces all her knowledge of natural fibres, skill of dressmaking, communication alongside her passion for the health of Mother Earth into becoming a pioneer. Advocating for conscious clothing and dressing to minimise the negative impacts on the environment, Jane has raised the awareness of natural fibres and upcycling, enriching their value and bringing about positive global change.

Early in her journey Jane recognised that regional communities have a strong connection to country and she leapt at opportunities to agitate for change at a grassroots level. Communities like Coolah in the heart of the New South Wales bush, were empowered and enthralled by Jane's passion and resurgence of values and skills to enhance conscious clothing.

Regional towns and local governments have been open-minded and receptive to uptake sustainable ways to influence positive change and reduce the negative impact clothing has on the environment. Jane's first solo exhibition was held at Coolah in conjunction with educative workshops. Our leadership connection has magnified positive change.

Ele Cook, ARLP colleague and organic beef producer, Coolah, New South Wales

1. Increasing

Photo by Victoria Nikolova,
St Margaret's Anglican Girls School

Great vibe at Tarndie after the Slow Clothing talk and workshop. We've found your visit highly motivating and feel your insight will have an impact here for a long time to come.

Tom Dennis, 'Tarndie', Colac, Victoria

Having worked as a journalist and media consultant, Jane had this strong advocacy background and run successful campaigns using all of those skills. Her Slow Clothing work is an amalgam of everything that Jane is, which makes for a strong campaign about sustainability, upcycling and changing attitudes. There's the nucleus of her philosophy and beliefs, there's the work with Sew it Again and there's her talks to change people's behaviours. Jane is an artist as well as an influencer and advocate, and all these things make her an influential campaigner for this particular idea. I think this is an incredible journey Jane's been on and I admire that she has been able to bring other people along with her.

Dr Kay Pearse, consultant, Brno, Czech Republic

Jane's passion and tenacity amaze and inspire. She has grown this movement quietly, confidently and with deft speed. Great work.

Jenny Woodward, fashion lover, op shop fan and ABC weather presenter, Queensland

Jane's work had a profound impact on me when I attended her workshop. My two sisters were similarly moved to action after attending her session at their local library. People like Jane are showing us how we can live in more sustainable ways—I am deeply appreciative of this.

Dr Jennifer Nayler, education consultant, Queensland

It was an absolute pleasure to have Jane in the classroom. The girls were enthralled by her philosophy and skill, and 100 per cent with her.

Nikki Anderson, secondary teacher, St Margaret's Anglican Girls School, Brisbane, Queensland

The roadmap of a jam-packed career not only has many highlights and achievements, but for Jane Milburn has also included evolution and transformation in her passion, experiences and engagement. We both started our professional life as enthusiastic agricultural graduates, when concepts such as sustainability were starting to be a focus and had a strong practical implication for agriculture. As a communications' specialist, Jane has had to focus on key messages and make a clear and digestible story.

Today all these factors come into play as Jane guides one through the practicality of sustainability in daily life – where the value and way we live can be part of a collective effort to better care for and treasure the world around us. Her cut-through manifesto on slow clothing is engaging and practical and demonstrates a leadership that is inspiring and invaluable to many. And if I was a young and emerging professional, Jane's approach to a sustainable and values-based livelihood would be impacting on my roadmap.

Dr Piet Filet – Knowledge and collaboration broker, Founder of Flood Community of Practice

There was quite a sense of wonder at your presentation. Your energy and enthusiasm are infectious. I felt there was a similar infectiousness at the workshop too.

Patti Foster, Creative Recycling Augusta, Western Australia

Jane Milburn's presentations are inspiring, as we discovered during her visit to the Australian Capital Territory. She places an emphasis on slow and ethical fashion backed up by hard facts.

Not only does Jane understand the theory of slowing down clothing consumption she has practised it. She demonstrates how she reworks garments once, twice, sometimes three times into something new. Old garments are seen as a resource, and shirts become skirts.

Jane Milburn has coined slogans to raise awareness about her work like 'Second-hand is the new organic' and 'Dressing is an agricultural act'.

Edwina Robinson, executive officer, SEE-Change, Australian Capital Territory

In a 2017 Making Do exhibition, Jane Milburn's History Skirt was teamed with an op shop-found linen shirt and a collar made from cotton t-shirt offcuts:

'There is a great irony that the making do once born of great need, is now born of enormous over-supply. In our society of increasing waste, artists and artisans are turning to recycling materials—including plastic and clothing—to explore the associated environmental concerns through their work.
This process can open up discussion and re-shape thinking about waste and its effects on the planet.'

– Making Do exhibition, Bribie Island Seaside Museum
   Courtesy of Moreton Bay Regional Council, Queensland

Give someone a shirt, they wear it for a season.
Teach someone to sew,
they are clothed for a lifetime.

— Jane Milburn

NO
IMPORTS
No new pests and diseases
Safe Australian food
www.abgc.org.au

Jane upcycled her earlier
banana imports campaign
t-shirt using a Natalie
Chanin camisole pattern
with hand-stitching

✄ 2011 ✄
- ♥ preloved Fashion for Flood fundraiser
- ♥ begin noticing fashion excess

✄ 2012 ✄
- ♥ return to upcycling garments
- ♥ make first History Skirt

✄ 2013 ✄
- ♥ postgraduate study
- ♥ launch Textile Beat
- ♥ went public with wearing secondhand
- ♥ host first upcycling workshops

✄ 2014 ✄
- ♥ Sew it Again project, 365 daily upcycles
- ♥ first conference speech
- ♥ preloved bloggers go mainstream
- ♥ exhibit at Pandora Gallery, Coolah, NSW

✄ 2015 ✄
- ♥ create Slow Clothing Manifesto
- ♥ publish first HEIA journal paper
- ♥ refashion at Reverse Garbage Queensland
- ♥ begin library workshops on Slow Clothing

✄ 2016 ✄
- ♥ The Slow Clothing Project
- ♥ Revive with Brisbane City Council
- ♥ host upcycling workshops for teachers
- ♥ learn new skills in Japan

✄ 2017 ✄
- ♥ first keynote address
- ♥ national TV coverage for clothing issues
- ♥ contribute to War on Waste
- ♥ TEDxQUT talk on Slow Clothing
- ♥ History Skirt exhibited
- ♥ co-curate and co-MC Worn OUT?!?
  refashion at Reverse Garbage Queensland
- ♥ produce Slow Clothing, the book

Jane Milburn in the Textile Beat studio.
Photo by Fiona Lake.

REFERENCES

Books

Andrew Brooks, *Clothing poverty: The hidden world of fast fashion and second-hand clothes*, Zed Books, 2015

Annika Sanders and Kerry Seager, *Junky styling: Wardrobe surgery.* A & C Black Publishers Ltd, 2009

Clare Press, *Wardrobe crisis: How we went from Sunday best to fast fashion*, Nero, 2016

Daniel Pink, *A Whole New Mind* Riverhead Books, 2005

Deepak Chopra, *The seven spiritual laws of superheroes*, Transworld Publishers Ltd, 2013

Eckhart Tolle, *A New Earth: Awakening to your life's purpose*, The Penguin Group, Australia, 2005

Edward De Bono, *Think! Before it's too late*, Bolinda Publishing, 2012

Elizabeth Cline, *Overdressed: The Shockingly High Price of Cheap Fashion*, Penguin Putnam, 2013

Ellen Langer, *On becoming an artist*, Random House USA Inc, 2006

Garry Egger and Boyd Swinburn, *Planet Obesity*, Allen & Unwin, 2010

Isabelle Thomas & Frédérique Veysset, *Paris Street Style: A guide to effortless chic,* Abrams Image, 2013

Judi Ketteler, *Sew Retro: A stylish history of the sewing revolution*, Voyageur Press, 2010

Julian Cribb, *The coming famine*, CSIRO Publishing, 2010

Julie Paterson, *ClothBound*, Murdoch Books, 2015

Juliet Schor, *True Wealth*, Penguin Group, 2011, pg 28

Kate Fletcher, *Sustainable Fashion and Textiles: Design Journeys*, Routledge, 2014, pg 222

Katherine Wilson,*Tinkering: Australians reinvent DIY culture,* Monash University Publishing, 2017

Keelen Mailman, *The Power of Bones*, Allen & Unwin, 2014

Lucy Siegle, *To die for: Is fashion wearing out the world?*, Fourth Estate, 2011

Marie Kondo, *The life-changing magic of tidying up,* Ten Speed Press, 2014

Matilda Lee, *Eco chic: The savvy shoppers guide to ethical fashion*, Octopus Books, 2007

Michael Pollan, *In Defence of Food*, Penguin Books, 2008

Misao Jo & Kenzo Jo, *SAORI: Self-innovation through free weaving, Saorinomori.* 2012 pg 135

Naomi Klein, *This changes everything*, Simon & Schuster, 2014

Richard Denniss, *Curing Affluenza: How to buy less stuff and save the world*, Black Inc, 2017

Sass Brown, *Eco fashion*, Laurence King Publishing, 2010

Sass Brown, *Refashioned*, Laurence King Publishing, 2013

Stephen Boyden, *The Biology of Civilisation: Understanding human culture as a force in nature*, UNSW, 2004

Weblinks <superscript/>current at November 2017

[1] http://www.mckinsey.com/business-functions/sustainability-and-resource-productivity/our-insights/style-thats-sustainable-a-new-fast-fashion-formula?cid=sustainability-eml-alt-mip-mck-oth-1610

[2] http://www.innovationintextiles.com/automated-sewbot-to-make-800000-adidas-tshirts-daily/?sthash.hakeXKPj.mjjo

[3] Browne, M. (2011). Accumulation of microplastic on shorelines worldwide: Sources and sinks. Environmental Science and Technology, 45 (21), 9175–9179.

[4] https://orbmedia.org/stories/Invisibles_plastics

[5] https://www.copenhagenfashionsummit.com/pulse/

[6] Milburn, J (2016) Valuing old skills in a new world, Journal of the HEIA, Vol 23, No 2

[7] http://theconversation.com/an-official-welcome-to-the-anthropocene-epoch-but-who-gets-to-decide-its-here-57113

[8] https://dairygood.org/content/2017/survey-some-americans-think-chocolate-milk-comes-from-brown-cows

[9] https://www.ecoliteracy.org/article/wendell-berry-pleasures-eating

[10] https://www.foodconnect.com.au/

[11] Australian Institute of Health and Welfare. (2012). Australian Health Survey. Retrieved 1 November 2017 from http://www.aihw.gov.au/overweight-and-obesity/

[12] ABC. (2014). The men who made us fat (2014). BBC documentary by Jacques Peretti, Series 1 Episode 3. Retrieved 1 November 2017 from http://www.abc.net.au/tv/programs/men-who-made-us-fat/

[13] New Scientist. (2014, March 30). Our stuff: Why it's human nature to own things. Retrieved 31 May 2015 from http://www.newscientist.com/special/stuff

[14] Source: ABS, CommSec and Alan Kohler, October 2017

[15] Castle, J. (2014). Where did you get that outfit? Choice magazine, July 2014. Retrieved 1 November 2017 from https://www.choice.com.au/shopping/everyday-shopping/clothing/articles/ethical-clothing

[16] http://news.bio-based.eu/fiber-year-top-ten-producing-countries-2005-2013-2020/

[17] http://www.mckinsey.com/business-functions/sustainability-and-resource-productivity/our-insights/style-thats-sustainable-a-new-fast-fashion-formula?cid=sustainability-eml-alt-mip-mck-oth-1610

[18] Browne, M., Crump, P., Niven, S., Teuten, E., Tonkin, A., Galloway, T., et al. (2011). Accumulation of microplastic on shorelines woldwide: Sources and sinks. Environmental Science and Technology, 45 (21), 9175–9179.

[19] Articulated at Microplastics: A Macro Problem session, World Science Festival, March 2017, Brisbane

[20] https://portals.iucn.org/library/sites/library/files/documents/2017-002.pdf

[21] https://orbmedia.org/stories/Invisibles_plastics

[22] https://www.newscientist.com/article/mg23531380-500-back-to-the-wild-how-nature-is-reclaiming-farmland/

[23] Roth, G. (2014). Australian grown cotton sustainability report 2014. Cotton Australia & Cotton Research and Development Corporation. Retrieved 1 November 2017 from http://cottonaustralia.com.au/uploads/publications/Sustainability_report_201114.PDF

[24] Trindall, J., Roth, G., Williams, S., Wigginton, D., & Harris, G. (Eds.) (2012). The Australian cotton water story: A decade of research & development 2002–12.

[25] http://www.global-standard.org/certification.html

[26] https://oecotextiles.wordpress.com/2014/10/15/climate-change-and-the-textile-industry/

[27] https://goodonyou.eco/material-guide-viscose-really-better-environment/

[28]http://www.abc.net.au/news/2014-04-24/australian-clothing-retailers-yet-to-sign-factory-safety-accord/5408028

[29]http://fashionrevolution.org/about/

[30]https://baptistworldaid.org.au/resources/2017-ethical-fashion-report/

[31]http://ethicalclothingaustralia.org.au/

[32]https://goodonyou.eco/app/

[33]http://www.barnardos.org.uk/news/media_centre/Once-worn-thrice-shy-8211-British-women8217s-wardrobe-habits-exposed/press_releases.htm?ref=105244

[34]H&M. (2015). Conscious Actions Sustainability Report 2015. Retrieved 1 November 2017 from http://sustainability.hm.com/content/dam/hm/about/documents/en/CSR/2015%20Sustainability%20report/HM_SustainabilityReport_2015_final_FullReport_en.pdf

[35]Conversations between Australia local governments and the author

[36]http://cdn1.blockassets.com/assets/tfia/press-releases/6z7ifJMLWqZD90T/Stain-Removal-TFIA-media-release-30-September.pdf

[37]Australian Bureau of Statistics. (2013). 4655.0.55.002—Information paper: Towards the Australian environmental-economic accounts, Chapter 4. Retrieved 9 November 2016 from http://www.abs.gov.au/ausstats/abs@.nsf/Products/4655.0.55.002~2013~Main+Features~Chapter+4+Waste?OpenDocument

[38]http://www.nacro.org.au/policy/

[38]NACRO information sourced from the Australian Bureau of Statistics

[39]The Economist. (2016). Government takes aim at well-meaning foreigners. The Economist, April 2016. Retrieved 9 November 2016 from http://www.economist.com/news/middle-east-and-africa/21695877-government-takes-aim-well-meaning-foreigners-let-them-weave-their-own

[40]Aeon. (2016). Unravel. Retrieved 1 November 2017 from https://aeon.co/videos/this-is-the-final-resting-place-of-your-cast-off-clothing

[41]WRAP. (2012). Valuing our clothes: The true cost of how we design, use and dispose of clothes in the UK. Retrieved 1 November 2017 from http://www.wrap.org.uk/content/valuing-our-clothes

[43]http://www.wrap.org.uk/content/landfill-falls-out-fashion-uk-embraces-sustainable-clothing

[44]http://www.wrap.org.uk/sites/files/wrap/valuing-our-clothes-the-cost-of-uk-fashion_WRAP.pdf#page=10

[45]http://textilebeat.com/wp-content/uploads/2015/11/speech-and-response_24_nov_2015.pdf

[46]http://textilebeat.com/revive-style-for-planetary-health/

[47]http://textilebeat.com/helping-divert-textiles-from-landfill/

[48]Ward, A. (2012). It's a stitch up! How seven out of 10 young people don't know how to sew a button. Daily Mail, October 2012. Retrieved 1 November 2017 from http://www.dailymail.co.uk/news/article-2213723/Young-adults-useless-basic-tasks.html

[49]http://www.bbc.co.uk/programmes/b03myqj2 Retrieved 1 November 2017

[50]Norum, P. (2013). Examination of apparel maintenance skills and practices: Implications for sustainable clothing consumption. Family and Consumer Sciences Research Journal, 42 (2), 124–137.

[51]http://www.mudjeans.eu/

[52]https://www.citizenwolf.com/

[53]https://www.vogue.com/article/viktor-and-rolf-spring-2017-couture-upcycled-vintage-gowns-behind-the-scenes

[54]Orange, R. (2016). Waste not want not: Sweden to give tax breaks on repairs. The Guardian, September 2016. September 2016. Retrieved 1 November 2017 https://www.theguardian.com/world/2016/sep/19/waste-not-want-not-sweden-tax-breaks-repairs

[55]http://www.cam.ac.uk/research/news/well-dressed

[56]WRAP. (2015). Extending the life of clothes. Retrieved 1 November 2017 from http://www.wrap.org.uk/content/extending-life-clothes#sthash.YfQpZxn2.dpuf

[57]Sew it Again. (2016). Retrieved 1 November 2017 from www.sewitagain.com

[58]http://victorylamour.com/why-im-learning-to-sew/

[59]http://trove.nla.gov.au/work/9644299?selectedversion=NBD3181161

[60]Attributed to Donald H McGannon, a US broadcasting industry executive

[61]http://www.milburnmedia.com/Food-Farming-Australia.pdf

[62]https://croakey.org/whats-on-the-menu-for-queenslands-new-health-media-club-some-ministerial-grilling-perhaps/

[63]https://blueandwhitetokyo.com/2014/10/21/crazy-sashiko-2/

[64]https://www.truity.com/personality-type/INFP

[65]https://blog.mraconsulting.com.au/2016/04/20/state-of-waste-2016-current-and-future-australian-trends/

[66]Attributed to American athlete Arthur Ashe

[67]http://philippschmidt.org/articles/2016-Schmidt-Resnick-Ito.pdf

[68]http://juliepaterson.com.au/product/clothbound/

[69]https://espace.curtin.edu.au/handle/20.500.11937/1629

[70]https://soundcloud.com/612abcbrisbane/sew-it-again-a-365-day-eco-clothing-project

[71]https://www.youtube.com/watch?v=NYqiLJBXbss

[72]https://www.brainyquote.com/quotes/authors/a/albert_einstein.html

[73]http://sustainable-fashion.com/projects/local-wisdom/

[74]https://www.theguardian.com/sustainable-business/sustainable-fashion-blog/gallery/2014/apr/04/our-relationship-with-clothes-in-pictures

[75]http://www.edelkoort.com/

[76]http://about.abc.net.au/2014/07/life-mirrors-life-series/

[77]https://www.ruralpressclub.com.au/content/previous-winners

[78]http://www.thelancet.com/commissions/planetary-health

[79]http://www.oxfam.org.uk/media-centre/press-releases/2016/06/over-three-billion-clothes-left-unworn-in-the-nations-wardrobes-survey-finds

[80]https://www.dosomethingnearyou.com.au/articles/media/new-research-national-op-shop-week-2013

[81]https://truecostmovie.com/

[82]http://www.wikihow.com/Dress-Indie

[83]https://bodyimagemovement.com/

[84]http://www.colormebeautiful.com/seasons/findyourseason.html

[85]https://truecostmovie.com/learn-more/buying-better/

[86]https://www.ncbi.nlm.nih.gov/pmc/articles/PMC4249026/#B10

[87]https://goodonyou.eco/material-guide-viscose-really-better-environment/

[88]http://shrinkthatfootprint.com/how-big-is-a-house

[89]https://bemorewithless.com/project-333/

[90]https://fiftythings2016.wordpress.com/author/pamelajgreet/

[91]http://www.huffingtonpost.com.au/2017/04/02/psychologists-explain-the-benefits-of-baking-for-other-

people_a_22022154/?utm_hp_ref=au-homepage&amp%3Bncid=fcbklnkauhpmg00000001

[92]http://knitting.diyeverywhere.com/2016/09/15/what-knitting-is-doing-to-your-health-that-you-probably-never-knew-about-/?src=share_fb_new_56025&t=syn

[93]https://www.instagram.com/fayedelanty/

[94]https://www.instagram.com/nevereverpayretail/

[95]https://www.instagram.com/drossintogold/

[96]https://www.instagram.com/theonlywayisop/

[97]https://www.instagram.com/unmaterialgirl/

[98]https://www.instagram.com/jonathan_pampling/

[99]http://boomerangbags.org/

Other reading

Beverly Gordon, *Textiles: the whole story,* Thames & Hudson Ltd, 2013

Dawn O'Porter, *This Old Thing*, Hot Key Books, London, 2014

India Flint, *Eco Colour : Environmentally Sustainable Dyes,* Murdoch Books, 2008

India Flint, *Second Skin*, Murdoch Books, 2011

Julia Cameron, *The artist's way,* Souvenir Press Ltd, 2007

Julie Paterson, *ClothBound: stories of a handmade process*, Murdoch Books, Australia, 2015

Kate Black, *Magnifeco your head-to-toe guide to ethical fashion*, New Society Publishers, Canada, 2015

Natalie Chanin, *Alabama Stitch Book: projects and stories celebrating hand-sewing*, HNA Books, New York, 2008

Nicole Jenkins, *Style is Eternal*, Melbourne University Publishing, Melbourne, 2014

Redress, *Dress with Sense*, Thames & Hudson, 2017

Safia Minney, *Slow Fashion, aesthetics meets ethics*, New Internationalist, 2016

Sandy Black, *The sustainable fashion handbook*, Thames & Hudson Ltd, 2012

Sheila Heti et al, *Women in Clothes*, Penguin, New York, 2014

Websites

Fashion Revolution http://fashionrevolution.org/

Eco Fashion Talk http://www.ecofashiontalk.com/

Alabama Chanin https://alabamachanin.com/

Junky Styling https://www.youtube.com/watch?v=-Fpi6YjY9W0

Local Wisdom http://www.localwisdom.info/about

The Slow Clothing Project http://textilebeat.com/slow-clothing/

Ecofashion Sewing http://www.ecofashionsewing.com/

Acknowledgements

Nothing is created in isolation. We grow and change based on what we know and have experienced. In this way, many people have helped and influenced my journey to Slow Clothing.

This book would not have happened without the stewardship of Heather Grant-Campbell and Belinda Pollard—thank you for your guidance, support and belief in me. Thank you to Julie Hillier and Elizabeth Kingston for friendship and styling assistance. Also thanks to Helen Kelly for graphics and illustrations.

My work has been made possible by encouragement and philanthropy from my family—including husband Darcy, our children Lily, Max and Casey and their partners Fi, Steph and Jenna. A particular thanks to Jenna (and grandbaby Ryan), for designing and guiding this publication.

I thank my brother Tony Capon for mentorship and his wife Dr Wendy Relf and my sister Joanne Seccombe for proofreading—as well as a lifetime of friendship. We also miss and remember our late brother Paul Capon for his love, care and resourcefulness. Wisdom from my mother-in-law, Granny Milburn, as well as my Great Grandma and Nana, Mum Elizabeth and Dad Phillip, and Aunt Kate McLachlan contributed to my capacity to write this book and I am deeply grateful to them for that.

Along the way, I have been influenced and supported in this work by Australian Rural Leadership Foundation colleagues—particularly Ele Cook, Georgie Somerset, Keelen Mailman, Carol Watson, Caroline Rhodes, Dr Jennifer Andrew, Barb Grey and Dr Sharon Downes.

I thank the many people who have encouraged the organic growth of my journey including friends, colleagues, teachers, journalists, students, sustainability organisations, creative groups and local governments. I thank ABC broadcaster Rebecca Levingston for the 2013 radio interview which launched my upcycling journey and Dominique Tan from Biloela for enabling the first regional upcycling workshop. Thanks also to Kerrie Richards and Meriel Chamberlin for their natural-fibre expertise, and Dr Kay Pearse for mentoring.

I thank all the wonderful makers who contributed to The Slow Clothing Project as well as two talented women, India Flint and Natalie Chanin, who have made a valuable contribution to the thinking and actions of people, like myself, seeking more engaged ways of dressing.

Published by Textile Beat
Box 100
Toowong Q 4066
Brisbane, Queensland, Australia
www.textilebeat.com

Credits:
Words, concept and content by Jane Milburn
Design by Jenna Milburn
Editing by Heather Grant-Campbell
Artwork by Helen Kelly
Cover artwork by Belinda Pollard, with styling by Julie Hillier
Mannequin styling by Elizabeth Kingston
Photographs by Jane Milburn, Darcy Milburn, Fiona Lake, Patria Jannides, Dan Fidler, Tim Swinson, Russell Fisher, Caroline Rhodes, Shellie Buckle, Col Jackson, Chrissy Maguire, Kenzo Jo, Victoria Nikolova
Printed by IngramSpark, Melbourne

ISBN 978-0-6481817-0-5

CPSIA information can be obtained
at www.ICGtesting.com
Printed in the USA
LVHW071602201221
706739LV00007B/253